Iron Fist, Lead Foot:

John Coletti and Ford's "Terminator"

SVT
POWER!

FRANK

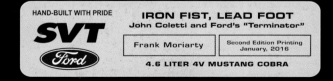

HAND-BUILT WITH PRIDE

SVT
Ford

IRON FIST, LEAD FOOT
John Coletti and Ford's "Terminator"

Frank Moriarty

Second Edition Printing
January, 2016

4.6 LITER 4V MUSTANG COBRA

Frank Moriarty

T-5 DESIGN

ISBN-13: 978-0-9754360-6-6

Iron Fist, Lead Foot: John Coletti and Ford's "Terminator" is produced by T-5 Design LLC, Montoursville, Pennsylvania.

The information in this publication is true and complete to the best of our knowledge. All recommendations are made without any guarantee on the part of the authors or publisher, who also disclaim any liability incurred in connection with the use of this data. The author recognizes that some words, model names, and designations, for example, mentioned herein are the property of the trademark holder. They are used herein for identification purposes only. Every effort has been made by the author to ensure permission has been obtained and proper credit is given regarding the use of any photographs or illustrations that appear in this publication.

Unless otherwise noted, all photos are courtesy of Ford Motor Company.

Layout and design by Marcie A. Cipriani.

Printed in Malaysia.

DEDICATION

This book is dedicated to the workers of Ford Motor Company's Dearborn Assembly Plant, who built thousands upon thousands of Ford Mustangs.

When this massive facility closed on May 10, 2004, it brought an end to more than forty years of Mustang production at DAP. By the time it was phased out, the plant was considered outdated – to walk its passages was to pass through a dark, multi-layered labyrinth. Yet one thing was certain: that huge building, first opened in 1918, felt historic. And in the world of American manufacturing, it was.

On the surface, life in DAP appeared chaotic, but in its own way the plant was extremely orderly. It was simply a case where processes and procedures required adaptation to fit within DAP's unconventional environment, one that had evolved over eight decades of manufacturing. But every conversation I had with the members of Ford's Special Vehicle Team was characterized by unsolicited praise for the excitement and dedication of DAP's workers. I feel fortunate to have had the chance to spend several days at the plant to see this devotion for myself.

For the workers at DAP, building Mustangs and Cobras was a job. But, from what I saw, every single aspect was truly done with pride.

Official Licensed Product

ACKNOWLEDGEMENTS

In my experience writing about racing and high performance vehicles, I've found there's something about the enthusiasm of people who work with and love cars that gives an author a certain added boost and encouragement. In the case of this book, thanks for that energy must begin with a spin around the Ford world.

Within Ford's Special Vehicle Team, some engineers spoke informally or without attribution, while others were kind enough to take time from their schedules to sit down for formal interviews and a host of follow-up calls. Among the latter, thanks to Scott Tate, Mike Luzader, Dave Dempster, Brian Roback, Nick Terzes, Celeste Kupczewski, Enzo Campagnolo, and Jeff Grauer. Dave Diegel made a trip into the SVT offices so we could talk, while Primo Goffi and Tom Bochenek generously set aside time even when the looming target date of the Ford GT program was demanding their attention. Tom Scarpello provided insight from his vantage point, Bob Lewis gave an overview of the SVT dealer networks, and Camilo Pardo dug through his design files to show me faces the Terminator might have had. Tom Chapman demonstrated things I never knew a Terminator could do as we thundered around the Dearborn Proving Ground Handling Course, devouring a set of tires in the process. Unforgettable!

Of course, none of the above could have happened without the support of Alan Hall, who so professionally coordinated SVT media activities while displaying a fan's sense of appreciation about the team's work. Thanks also to Alan's associates Jayson Demchak and Monty Doran, who shepherded me here and there within Ford's facilities.

At Dearborn Assembly Plant, Tommy Demeester and Al Frank showed me why people said they knew everything there was to know about DAP. I'll never forget the time I spent with them, and I came away with even greater appreciation of the vehicles that have been crafted at DAP.

At Romeo Engine Plant, Gerry Klandrud opened so many doors for me, and made sure I not only saw the Niche Line, but got a tour of the general plant activities as well. Mike Eller envisioned the idea of the Niche Line, and helped me understand how its development came about before turning me over to Bob McIntyre and Ron Anderson, who answered my questions as they built a Terminator engine with the pride and care that have made the Niche Line famous. Cary Kramp, Brad Lammers, and Tom Wilson then gave me insight into how great an impact the Terminator had on Romeo Engine and how some impossible demands were made possible after all.

I also appreciate Bill Ford taking the time to answer my questions about SVT and the Terminator, and Tom Hoyt at Ford World Headquarters for facilitating this interview.

Outside of the Ford sphere, Michael Tokarchik at Manley Performance Products and Mark Dipko, who departed SVT after performing vital initial work on the last of the SVT Mustang Cobras, gave accounts of their important Terminator contributions. Thanks also to Mike Pakoskey.

John Maffucci passed along images of his Land Speed Record Cobra, and Nick Twork, who was in the right place at the right time, camera in hand, allowed me to use one of the most famous of all Terminator photographs.

It was a feature in the fifteenth anniversary issue of *Muscle Mustangs and Fast Fords* that led directly to this book, and I thank Jim Campisano for getting behind the feature idea right away, making the rest of the project possible.

Darin Kreiss at Maguire's Ford in Duncannon, Pennsylvania supplied me with his opinions and thoughts, as well as my very own Terminator. The former were freely-given, the latter… Well, it was worth it!

Alan Sciscio was that most valuable of proofreaders – someone interested in the subject, but with a sharp eye for details. Dan Taylor and John Taylor also provided advice and perspective.

Without the support, advice, and energy of John Clor this book might not have reached the bookshelves of the world – thank you, John.

Rich Wenzke was kind enough to bring his immaculate 1931 Ford Model A over for a photo session with my Terminator on a hot summer day, and having that opportunity is tremendously appreciated. Rich's car is older, mine is faster, but they are both wonderful examples of different eras in Ford Motor Company's illustrious history.

If Joe Goffin isn't the Number One Fan of the Terminator I don't know who is. His enthusiasm for this book contributed to this edition in so many ways, and his website is a Terminator treasure trove: www.terminator-cobra.com

Without Marcie Cipriani at T-5 Design this edition of this book likely never would have happened. It was a multi-year effort, but we finally made it happen. Marcie's sense of design makes this book something I hope all Terminator fans will treasure, and she was a great creative partner.

On the home front, my wife Leigh Anne yet again endured months of her husband obsessively laboring away when he wasn't suddenly jetting off to Detroit. To her, love and gratitude.

Finally, thanks to John Coletti, for overseeing the creation of some amazing vehicles – and proving that the hot rod guy isn't an extinct species after all.

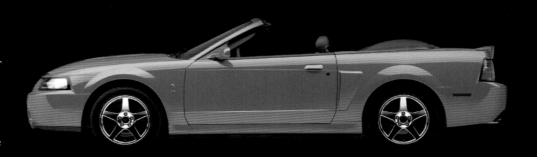

CONTENTS

Foreword by O. John Coletti : Director, Ford Special Vehicle Team

SPECIAL FEATURE : **BIRTH OF A COBRA**

FOREWORD

By O. John Coletti
Director, Ford Special Vehicle Team

To truly appreciate a car like the 2003-04 SVT Mustang Cobra, you first need to appreciate the concept behind the Ford Special Vehicle Team. As a real, cross-functional, enthusiast-focused "skunkworks" operation, Ford SVT was a highly unusual group within the traditional U.S. automotive industry.

It would have been virtually impossible for us to develop segment-leading performance vehicles within the mainstream environment. That's because the high-volume mainstream world is geared to develop products for a wide range of customers – buyers who need a vehicle to suit all or most of their transportation needs. Their purchase decision focuses on, "How do I get the most vehicle for my transportation dollar?"

But Ford SVT's focus was squarely on the enthusiast customer – buyers whose purchase decision has very little to do with "need" and very much to do with "want." To entice these influential and often high-profile buyers with "got-to-have" products, we had to develop the slickest, coolest vehicles that were the best-performing, best-handling, best-braking, etc. – attributes that turn drivers on and get their enthusiast juices flowing.

The unique business practices of the SVT operation were set up to most efficiently and effectively address the market-driven need to develop specialty products designed to satisfy the exclusive performance wants of the enthusiast customer. It was that laser-sharp focus that helped the last SVT Mustang Cobra – known internally as the "Terminator" program – not just meet, but to far exceed, its performance expectations.

In the mainstream, making a good product is a real accomplishment. But you need a great product to move the needle in the performance world. That's why we took so many risks with the Terminator program. We spent a lot of time developing a 2002 Cobra that turned out to be only marginally better in performance than the 2001 Cobra. In fact, the day we got back from our "Western Drive" performance evaluation trip, we all felt that the naturally aspirated prototype just wasn't going to get the job done. We knew that to get the upgraded performance we wanted, we would need to employ technology that had never been used on a production Mustang – supercharging the engine. So we were faced with two choices: 1.) Drop the SVT Cobra car line completely until the S197 Mustang hit the street; or 2.) Go for broke and build a supercharged Cobra.

When we got the team together and discussed our choices, everyone to a person voted to go for broke. To their credit, they took on the challenge and said let's just go ahead and build the fastest production Mustang Cobra ever. Credit for naming the program "Terminator" goes to Tom Bochenek, the Cobra program manager. It came during a discussion about any possible competition for the car. Although there had been rumors floating around Detroit for some time that GM was going to drop the F-body, we wanted to be prepared if they kept the car in production. We knew that a supercharged Cobra would "terminate" the Camaro-Mustang war once and for all. So "Terminator" it was.

Opposite: The first promotional photographs of the 2003 SVT Mustang Cobra captured the excitement of Terminators thundering down the open road.
Photo: Ford Motor Company

The Ford Special Vehicle Team was a special place to work. Not only did SVT have some of the best people in the business developing our products, they also had the heart and desire to build the best. Once we made the decision to go for broke, I was never worried that the team wouldn't get the job done. To use an old military adage, when you're going to war, you better have three things if you expect to win: 1.) Willpower; 2.) Staying power; and 3.) Firepower. I can tell you that SVT was blessed with an over-abundance of all three.

The people and the process behind SVT proved a key enabler for Terminator. If we had tried to develop this car following mainstream practices and then asked for "permission" to build the Terminator Cobra in the timeframe we had faced, it would have taken years, and the answer would have surely been, "It's too risky." We chose to go for it and ask for forgiveness later. Fortunately, the program came off with no forgiveness required.

Truly the "Terminator" Cobra stands as a benchmark in the history of Mustang performance, and as an example of SVT's unique value to Ford. SVT set out to build the best-performing Mustang Cobra ever – and we did. Since there isn't a production Mustang in the history of the car line that can beat the Terminator's overall performance, we set a new high-water mark. I just hope that all future Cobras are even better.

O. John Coletti
July, 2006

PREFACE

In 1992, while working on a book about the development of the Dodge Charger Daytona and Plymouth SuperBird, I had the opportunity to visit Chrysler's beautiful Technology Center in Auburn Hills, MI. Several of the key aerodynamicists who had worked on the legendary "wing car" program in the late 1960s still worked at Chrysler – John Pointer, Dick Lajoie, and Gary Romberg – and they had invited me to visit the massive facility.

Gary Romberg was about to show me the center's scale wind tunnel, but first had to duck in and make sure nothing related to their current project was visible. That project was the aerodynamic study of the Dodge pickup trucks that would not hit the market for another four to five years.

Lead time measured in years is common in the auto industry. The complexity of designing, engineering, and then building a new vehicle is imposing.

When the 2003 SVT Ford Mustang Cobra arrived on the scene in early 2002 to media raves and public acclaim, I assumed it was the product of a long and thoughtful process. It turns out that the process was anything but long – and though much thought by Ford's Special Vehicle Team engineers graced this vehicle, its birth was driven by the simple gut reaction of an auto industry legend, John Coletti.

The more I learned about the vehicle developed under the code name "Terminator," the more I realized there was a fascinating story here. The tale blossomed from a feature article in the fifteenth anniversary issue of *Muscle Mustangs and Fast Fords* magazine into this book.

In many ways, the story of the Terminator parallels the development of the Daytona and the SuperBird. Crushing deadlines, rapid advancements, inevitable dejection, and eventual triumph – these phases existed in both accounts. But where the Chrysler team had hauled their base vehicles out of the assembly process for their transformation into Daytonas and SuperBirds, Ford's Special Vehicle Team had to build their Cobras on the standard Mustang production line at Dearborn Assembly Plant. An assembly line is designed to do the same thing over and over. It does not like exceptions or customization – but building the Terminator demanded both. Without DAP's willingness to re-think a large part of their assembly process, there would have been no Terminator.

Still, there's no doubting that the very idea of a supercharged Cobra sprang from the stubborn determination of John Coletti. As the leader of SVT, Coletti possessed that one intangible quality that is precious and rare in the executive ranks, the ability to inspire. By all accounts there were times when he could be loud, angry, impatient – but those qualities paled in light of his talent for leading and inspiring SVT's talented staff in the creation of acclaimed new performance vehicles.

As you'll see in this story, with the Terminator Coletti made a radical decision for the simplest of reasons – because it was the right one. That choice caused headaches that rippled from the ranks of Ford's executives down to the dealerships that sold SVT products, and could have been avoided if Coletti had only been willing to accept "good enough." But it was not in his nature to make such a concession. In these days of timid management professionals, that's a standard to be wholeheartedly celebrated.

Looking back on the Terminator development program well over a decade later, it's clear to see that this realm of incredibly talented engineers, risk-taking executives, enthusiastic auto workers and engine builders, and a host of others came together in a unique synergy, the story of which still seems to vibrate and pulse with energy. Under tremendous pressure and in just a handful of months, they collaborated on the creation of what will be remembered as a classic high performance vehicle of its era. For that reason, I have elected to leave this story told mostly in the present tense, to let that energy resonate through the years.

Finally, like many books, the one you are holding is the realization of a creative vision. But it's a realization that was long delayed.

When I was first starting to write this book in 2003, I began researching my publishing options. I met a guy named Tom Shreiner, an incredible Mustang enthusiast and the author of a book I was well aware of, *The SVT Mustang Cobra Recognition Guide*. It turns out Tom was interested in moving into publishing, partnering with graphic designer Marcie Cipriani. It seemed like an ideal convergence of talents and resources that was meant to be.

The three of us began excitedly laying out my tale of the Terminator within the context of a large-format, full-color book containing hundreds of bright images. And then the darkest of clouds came with Tom losing his battle with cancer in July, 2005. I was forced to take my manuscript and issue it by any means at hand, the book eventually emerging in humble paperback with just a few poorly-reproduced black-and-white photos. Still, Terminator fans bought thousands of copies, and their warm words in letters and emails went a long way toward easing any disappointment over the lo-fi format.

Still, over the years Marcie and I had occasional contact in the Ford SVT world. And one day she brought up an interesting idea: what if we did a tenth anniversary edition of *Iron Fist, Lead Foot*, turning it into the book the three of us had imagined years ago?

So, really, there's only one thing left to say: Hey, Tom – we did it!

Frank Moriarty
July, 2015

Opposite:
The Terminator was a hit with the wind-in-the-hair crowd, as the convertible proved to be a popular choice among that segment of driving enthusiasts. The darker of the drop-tops seen here is painted with the unique color-shifting Mystichrome finish offered in 2004.
Photo: Ford Motor Company

CHAPTER 1 DESERT STORM

A Born Leader

Opposite: Just another Ford in the desert? Things are not always what they seem, with the American West offering ample and relatively deserted stretches of highway for long test drives of automotive prototypes. One such drive launched the entire Terminator program.

The forbidding desert of Nevada's Death Valley.

A barren landscape that could serve as the very definition of desolation would seem, on the surface at least, to have little reason to play a role in the creation of a modern muscle car. But when the vehicle in question is the 2003 Ford SVT Mustang Cobra – the manufacturer's flagship performance model – the unexpected frequently became the norm.

How did such a forsaken site – thousands of miles removed from both Ford's sprawling Dearborn, Michigan complexes and the secretive confines of the company's Special Vehicle Team facility – wind up playing host to the defining moment in the development program of one of the most amazing Mustangs in the iconic model's decades-long history?

The answer lies in the events of a warm afternoon late in the year 2000.

On that day, the desert stillness was suddenly broken by the howling roar of onrushing performance cars as SVT carried out its annual tradition known as the Western Drive.

Each year, the expanses of the American West provide the perfect setting for Ford's developers of high performance machinery to air out the latest vehicles to emerge from design studies and engineering exercises undertaken back home near Detroit. Many auto manufacturers take advantage of the ad hoc proving grounds afforded by the less-populated regions of California and Nevada, and Ford is no exception. Every member of SVT looks forward to the journey west just after each Labor Day.

Leading the charge across the expanse this day was none other than John Coletti – director of Ford's Special Vehicle Team and a man whose career has been inexorably linked with the Ford Mustang.

Employed by "the blue oval" for more than three decades, Coletti is an ideal figurehead for SVT, with master's degrees in both mechanical engineering and business administration. A respected member of the Society of Automotive Engineers since 1973, Coletti holds patents on automotive innovations he has developed.

But more importantly, Coletti is a born leader. His charismatic, no-nonsense approach has served him well. And in the 1990s, it saved the Ford Mustang.

With a misguided eye toward the future, Ford had planned to replace the classic rear-wheel drive Mustang with a front-drive model based on a Mazda platform. Coletti lobbied hard against the idea, and eventually the company relented, with the new vehicle arriving on the market as the Probe.

Coletti then set about revitalizing the faded glory of the Mustang, driving an efficient, largely secret program that resulted in the "SN95" 1994 Mustang. The near-unanimous acclaim that greeted the next-generation Mustang propelled Coletti into a new role as SVT's principal.

For Coletti, directing the programs of SVT is a hands-on job, and on that day in 2000 Coletti had his hands on the prototype of a planned 2002 SVT Mustang Cobra.

Ford's Special Vehicle Team making their annual Western Drive in 2001, the Mustangs clandestinely bearing the fruits of the Terminator development program.

Nevada's rustic Sourdough Saloon is about as different from Las Vegas glitz as you can get. The members of Ford's SVT were happy to add mementos to the automotive clutter lining the walls of the establishment.

While drivers and crew take a gas station break and pose for a group portrait on the 2001 Western Drive, the big boss of Ford's Special Vehicle Team, O. John Coletti, discovers his personal private parking location respectfully arranged by his team.

Opposite: Unlike the 2000 Western Drive, smiles abound among the SVT group as the Terminator technology is put through its paces in 2001. Note the coverings designed to disguise the new model's hood treatments.

While none of SVT's staff will deny that the Western Drive is fun, it is also a serious evaluation test. With Coletti ensconced behind the wheel of the new Mustang Cobra, there was no doubt everyone was anxious about their leader's reaction to his seat time in the next iteration of the Cobra. After all, raising the bar of performance is what the Mustang Cobra program is all about.

On its release, the Terminator would be the latest and greatest example of Mustang muscle, building on the proud heritage of the GT350 and the Boss 429 iterations that characterized the 1960's lineups.
Photos: Ford Motor Company

The Path to Performance

Performance was not necessarily the target more than forty years ago, when the Ford Mustang was introduced to the United States in television commercials on the eve of the car's official debut at the World's Fair in New York on April 17, 1964.

True, the little car had a sporty heritage, with its concept and development versions based on mid-engine sports car designs. But the Mustang that debuted in New York – and swept the nation with sales of 22,000 units on the first day of sale alone – came with a standard six-cylinder engine making just 101 horsepower.

Right off the bat, though, a 289 cubic inch displacement power plant found its way into the engine bay of America's new "Pony Car" – and the race was on.

Ample power to propel a light, smart handling car – this was the exciting characteristic that became the hallmark of the Mustang experience. And through the latter half of the 1960s, the Mustang became the host vehicle to some of the greatest creations of the muscle car era.

An alliance with Carroll Shelby in 1965 – a hot name in racing thanks to the success of his legendary Cobra sport cars – led to race-inspired Mustangs like the GT350 and the GT500. Other racing greats like South Carolina's Bud Moore, whose team featured drivers Parnelli Jones and George Follmer, also heeded the call of the Mustang. Moore's team achieved renowned road course victories with the 1970 Boss 302.

And then there was the Boss 429. Ford desperately needed a larger, more powerful engine for NASCAR competition in 1969 – and it had a 429 cubic inch solution in mind. NASCAR rules required at least 500 units of any given engine to be manufactured for street use, so Ford began shipping fastback Mustangs to its specialty contractor Kar Kraft, where the massive powerplant was shoehorned into the pony car's cramped engine bay. In truth, the mind-boggling torque and heavy engine of the Boss 429 program did not yield one of the better handling Mustangs, but there was no denying the awe factor.

Soon, though, insurance regulations and gas shortages conspired to bring about the death of the muscle car era. The Mustang heritage duly continued on in the 1970s and 1980s, but the awesome power of the 1960s was just a memory.

At least, that was the case until 1984. Earlier in the decade, Michael Kranefuss had been charged with developing Ford's new Special Vehicle Operations group. Envisioned as a way of returning a performance sheen to Ford's efforts, in 1984 SVO introduced its specialty Mustang. Though its turbocharged four-cylinder engine generated just 175 hp, features like a five-speed manual transmission with Hurst shifter, Traction-Lok rear axle, and large disc brakes contributed to a Mustang model that was received with delirious reviews in the automotive press.

The long performance famine was coming to an end. Indeed, it was SVO that served as a business model template for the formation of the Special Vehicle Team several years later. The birth of SVT in 1991 was also influenced by the success of Ford's European Special Vehicle Engineering team, which offered low-volume, high-performance cars like the Cosworth Escort.

Neil Ressler, Ford's director of vehicle engineering, was impressed by engineer Janine Bay's interest in a more potent Mustang, one easily tweaked with existing performance parts. Securing the support of Bob Rewey, executive vice president for sales and marketing, Ressler set up an American version of the SVE under Bay. Shortly after the tiny group

of seven official members was formed, the entity was christened the Special Vehicle Team.

The idea driving SVT's evolution throughout the 1990s was to draw together a small nucleus of engineers, product planners, and marketing experts in pursuit of four benchmarks of automotive excellence: Performance, Substance, Exclusivity, and Value. Engine, suspension, and braking refinement takes care of performance, while the team strives for built-in character to achieve substance. Via limited-production vehicles only available from a network of SVT-certified dealers, exclusivity is generated. But perhaps the biggest target of SVT is the value found in performance and driving pleasure, intangibles that outweigh the cost of the vehicles.

"Most Americans feel performance is an important vehicle attribute," Ford chairman and chief executive officer Bill Ford acknowledges. "SVT creates products for customers who are far more passionate about performance than the average person. So our SVT products become 'halo' vehicles for the entire Ford brand. When people see our SVT vehicles it gives them confidence that we'll have good performance in our other products."

Low-volume, high-performance cars were the basis of the entire SVT program, a business model used successfully in Europe, which offered vehicles such as the Cosworth Escort. The 1993 Mustang Cobra began the SVT family line.
Photos:
Bob D'Amato,
Ford Motor Company

When SVT celebrated its tenth anniversary in 2003, the team of less than fifty members was one of three key components in the Ford Performance Group, joining the competition-oriented Ford Racing Technology program and the Ford Racing Performance Parts retail distribution group.

"We think it's the best way," Bill Ford says of his company's small, specialized high performance group, "and other companies have copied our way of doing it, so I assume they think so, too. It takes enthusiasts to build vehicles that other enthusiasts are going to love.

"But it goes far beyond just creating products that we think a certain market segment will buy," Ford continues. "Ford Motor Company was born on a racetrack, with the investment money and publicity that my great-grandfather generated by racing. Performance is an important part of our heritage. SVT keeps that spirit alive inside the company. And the people who buy SVT vehicles are some of our greatest ambassadors outside the company. So SVT is really about maintaining the heart and soul of our company."

From the onset of SVT's efforts, the flagship of the team has been the Mustang Cobra. When Lee Iacocca sought a way to enhance the Mustang's performance credibility in the 1960's, the high-profile alliance with Carroll Shelby was the result. The recognition Shelby had generated racing the Ford-powered Cobra sports car was a valuable marketing tool, one that Ford recognized when they purchased the rights to combine the names "Cobra" and "Mustang."

Even after the Ford-Shelby alliance fell apart, the company occasionally mated snake and horse in an attempt to build a marketing buzz. The Mustang Cobra II model in the 1970s and "Fox body" Mustang Cobras in the early 1980s traded on the implication of performance inherent in the Cobra name, even if actual horsepower figures remained somewhat anemic.

But when SVT began its revitalization of the Mustang Cobra, there was more than a name behind the effort.

Introduced at the 1992 Chicago Auto Show, the 1993 Mustang Cobra was rated at 235 hp, although real world estimates place it at well over 250, primarily through he use of parts like Ford's GT40 intake manifold and cylinder heads. It was an enthusiastically-received first step, but SVT was just getting rolling.

Next up was the 1994-1995 model, officially rated at 240 hp and based on the newly-redesigned Mustang that John Coletti had fought so hard to bring into existence. This was followed by the 1996 Mustang Cobra which boosted horsepower to 305, a level that held steady through 1998. All was going well, as the team's logo came to signify increasing levels of performance. But in 1999 SVT hit its first speed bump. Though that year's Cobra became the first Mustang to boast an independent rear suspension, the vehicle's new intake and exhaust systems created an embarrassing situation: the production models made less horsepower than advertised. Though SVT took action to correct the situation, the planned 2000 Cobra was shelved, while the 2001 model offered only incremental improvements upon its release.

While these regular Mustang Cobras were impressive in their own right, SVT also labored to develop stripped-down, racing-oriented models christened Cobra Rs. Just 107 1993 Cobra R models were built, followed by the 250 white 351 cid 1995 models. But the Cobra R came into its own with the astonishing 2000 variation. Powered by a 385 hp 5.4-liter engine – compared to a stock Mustang GT's 4.6 liter at 260 hp – this pony was glued to the track by an imposing rear wing and ominous front profile crowned by a menacing air splitter.

With the 2000 Cobra R setting new standards for performance, SVT – just seven years after introducing its first Mustang Cobra – thought they were ready to take the next step. The plan was to create another naturally aspirated Mustang Cobra, a 2002 model that would mark a leap in performance over the 2001 edition just hitting the streets. It was this proposed 2002 model prototype that John Coletti found himself piloting on the Western Drive in September, 2000.

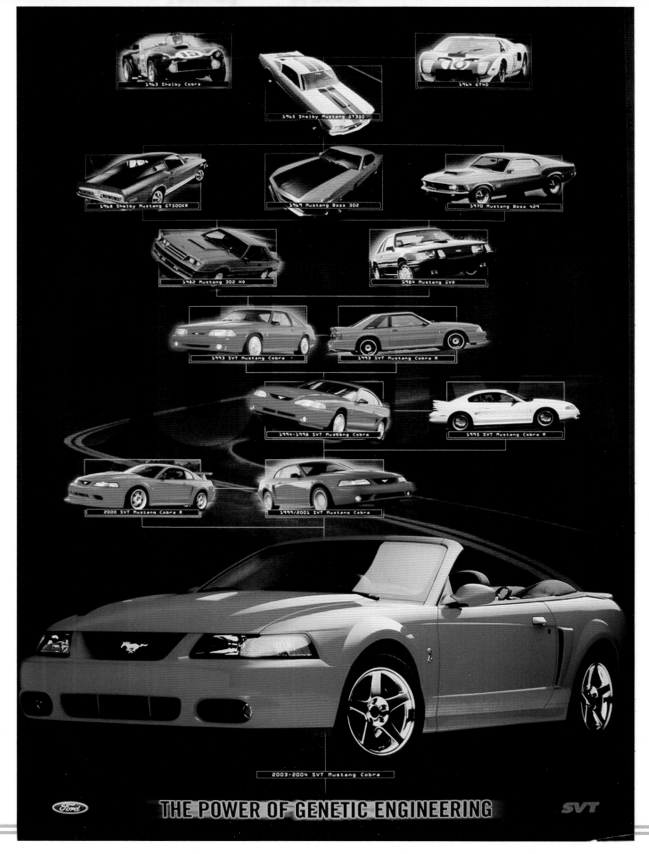

The mechanical genetic path that led to the Terminator is dramatically displayed in this Ford Motor Company promotional poster, but the real drama behind the development of the 2003-2004 SVT Mustang Cobra began on the troubled Western Drive of 2000.

An Ill Wind Blows

"What the hell's going on here?" John Coletti asked himself. He felt a sense of disbelief – and a growing swell of anger.

Behind the wheel of the big, bad Mustang Cobra, Coletti was thundering through the desert – and zipping just behind was a little Ford Focus, right on his tail. Granted, it was an SVT Focus, tweaked for power and handling, but SVT's boss was wheeling the big brother of the little compact. That Focus should have been eating dust.

No matter what Coletti did, the little car hung tough, like a mosquito buzzing around a tiger. And the longer the Focus stayed in his sight, the greater Coletti's agitation grew. This Mustang Cobra was supposed to be the flagship of SVT? This car that was having trouble dispatching a Ford Focus?

"It just didn't have any torque in higher gears," Coletti recalls. "In the lower gears it had more torque, but when you got up to the higher end? It just didn't have it."

At this critical moment there was little radio traffic on the frequency the SVT crew used for communication between cars on the Western Drive – except for the booming voice of the angry Coletti, that is.

"Nobody was even talking anymore on the radios," Coletti remembers, "because nobody wanted to hear me bitching any more – I'd just had it."

All too soon, it was time for a gas break in a tiny desert town. And time to face Coletti.

"So we get to Shoshone, and everybody's trying to stay away from me," Coletti readily admits. Primo Goffi, SVT engineer and Cobra team manager was an eyewitness.

"John's just got that mist in his face like he's ready to erupt," Goffi relates. "He's ready to come unglued. He said, 'You know guys, I'm going to go into this store and see if they sell any Alpo. And I'm going to buy a six-pack and throw it in the back seat of this thing because it's a dog. And I'm not going to associate myself with this thing because it is a dog.'"

On the spot, Coletti collared Tom Bochenek, Cobra program manager, and Bill Lane, powertrain engineering supervisor, in what has become known in SVT-lore as "the picnic table performance review."

"I grabbed Bochenek because he was the program manager and I grabbed Mr. Lane because he's the powertrain guy, and we began to… reason," Coletti says with exaggerated emphasis. "I told them, 'Guys, that's it – we ain't doing the program. That's no Cobra. Jesus Christ, it's an embarrassment – we ain't doing that car.'"

Coletti laughs now, but at the time he was beyond serious.

"I probably said a lot of other things," he admits. "The reason I know I was pissed is because I can't remember what I said! That's how pissed I was. Maniacal, you know? Because everybody remembers that part of it – and I don't!"

> "What the hell's going on here?" John Coletti asked himself. He felt a sense of disbelief – and a growing swell of anger.

CHAPTER 2 CLEARING THE PATH

"My point of view, frankly, was that all of the SVT vehicles would benefit by being developed by the same organization," Scarpello says. "In the case of the Cobra, in that time period from 1996 to 2001, the Cobra had actually been done by the mainstream Mustang group. So that wasn't pure in that sense, and authentic. So I was kind of the guy that was pushing John and trying to get him to take on the responsibility. And John, obviously like anyone, has concerns about resources, and you want to make sure you can do a good job," Scarpello continues. "So when we first talked about seriously making the change, and John now had the responsibility of the car, we talked about, 'Well, what is this first car going to be? What is it going to be like?'"

Eventually, it was mutually decided to simply enhance aspects of the 2001 model year Cobra for 2002, saving any radical revisions for Cobras of the future.

Marching Orders

Opposite: 2003 Cobra in Torch Red. Above: Initial plans for the 2002 Cobra were to enhance the naturally aspirated 2001 Cobra, shown here. The disappointing performance of the first 2002 prototype led to a complete overhaul of the Cobra program. *Photos: Ford Motor Company*

It would be safe to say that John Coletti provided the members of Ford's Special Vehicle Team with a bit more Western Drive feedback than they might have hoped. The impressions of SVT's boss from his seat time in the 2002 Mustang Cobra prototype came in loud and clear. And in colorful language, to boot.

Bluntly put, the new Cobra failed to meet Coletti's expectations. To make matters worse, the 2002 model was supposed to be a particularly important one for SVT. Ever since the mid-1990s, SVT's engineering efforts had been directed at concept and development vehicles. Though marketed by SVT, the 1996 through 2001 Cobras had actually been engineered by Team Mustang, the group that develops the mainstream Mustang products. But the planned 2002 Cobra was coming home to SVT, with every aspect of vehicle development under Coletti's domain.

Coletti had been encouraged to take on this additional responsibility by Tom Scarpello, who oversaw SVT's sales, marketing, and public relations efforts beginning in 1998. In many ways, SVT's direction throughout that era was a partnership between the two men.

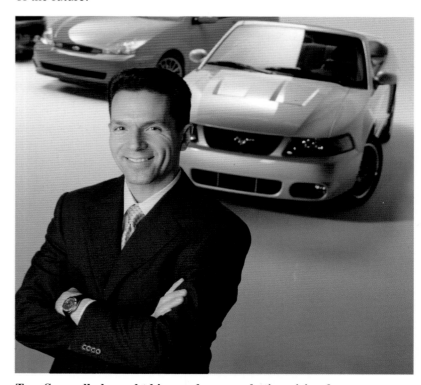

Tom Scarpello brought his own keen marketing vision from a background with Lincoln-Mercury and Ford of Mexico to Ford's Special Vehicle Team, a vision that meshed well with John Coletti's 'performance-at-all-costs' mantra.

"We were moving toward an evolutionary change as opposed to the revolutionary change that we all wanted," Scarpello admits. "It was a refinement issue, a decision that we felt still made the car a much better version of what the '01 was. It would have been naturally aspirated, probably 340 hp, a five-speed – you know, not too different from what the '01 Cobra was. And we went back and forth on that."

"We sat down with the marketing team prior to the trip and everybody said, what do we want for the next generation Cobra?" Coletti recalls of the weeks leading up to the Western Drive. "I'm thinking to myself, the new car's gotta be faster and better in every which way than the old car, the 2001 Cobra. So, we get together with the marketing guys and we start talking about what makes the best case. And we said, 'Well, we might be able to do a naturally aspirated car with around 340 hp' and try to keep the costs down, right?"

It was an admirable plan, and Coletti affirms, "I was fully behind the team's suggestion to go naturally aspirated." But in the universe of SVT, success is determined by performance. And the 2002 Cobra prototype was not performing.

As the fateful Western Drive drew to a close, the team assembled in Las Vegas to review the events of the long drive. Coletti's impressions had been made crystal clear, but he already had a solution in mind to snap shut the performance gap: supercharge the Cobra.

"I told them, 'Guys, unless you blow on this thing, we ain't doing this program. We're certainly not doing that car.'"

Coletti's pronouncement was met with a reaction that was not unexpected.

"Everybody was hemming and hawing – it can't be done, it can't be done, it's too short a time," Coletti recalls. "I said 'OK, guys, I'll tell you what – if what we're going to hear is a lot of whining out of you guys, let's just cancel the program now, fold up our tent, and go home.'"

The Impossible is Possible

"That was a decision to contemplate: whether we could supercharge or not," recalls Cobra team manager Primo Goffi. "I mean, that put us at the base of Mount Everest. That's bad enough, but the time frame that we were looking at, trying to get the car to the market…"

Goffi's uncertainty about the upheaval potentially caused by plans to supercharge the Cobra was shared by everyone at SVT. But there was no doubt that John Coletti had put a stake in the ground.

"Oh, yeh, I'm the stake slammer," Coletti readily admits. "My job is more like a coach than anything else. The team's all a bunch of great players; you just have to tell them, 'Here's what I'm expecting.'"

To illustrate the dynamic, Coletti refers to Bill Lane, the head of SVT's powertrain engineering.

"On every program that we've done, Bill's counseled me that it's too aggressive, we can't get there, it's impossible – 'John, you're asking us to do much more than we can possibly do.' It's like a broken record," Coletti smiles.

"But you know what? That's the initial speech. He gives me that and then what does he do? He makes it happen."

Returning to Michigan from the Western Drive, Coletti wanted to see his team figure out some way to equip the Cobra with the Model 90 supercharger from Eaton Automotive. But once again, Coletti's team surprised him.

"It was probably a week afterwards, and they'd kind of circled the wagon train," Coletti remembers. "And then they came in here with a proposal that said no, we want to put the Eaton 112 on there – the big one. So, they went from, 'I can't do this' – with what I considered a more modest power boost – to, 'Let's go with the whole enchilada!' I said, 'Hey, I'm with you guys!'"

With a new goal in SVT's collective mind, there was still a nagging question to be answered: could the radically revised program be pulled off from a practical standpoint?

2001 COBRA

2003-2004 COBRA

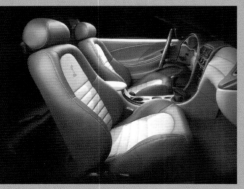

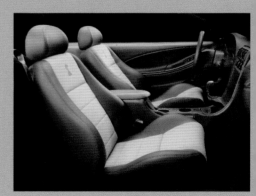

Dealers "Bought in" to the SVT Program

The presence of every Terminator that hit the streets was made possible by one critical role – a dealership's SVT salesperson. Darin Kreiss is a performance car enthusiast, an accomplished road racer, and a man who has sold more than his share of Ford Motor Company products. When Terminator mania was at its peak, some dealerships added "premiums" in the thousands of dollars over and above list price; instead, Darin and his dealership played fair and earned the respect of many performance car buyers – including your author, who ordered his 2003 SVT Mustang Cobra through Kreiss. Still active at Maguire's Ford in Duncannon, PA – and still owner of his own Terminator – Kreiss looks back on Ford's SVT sales program, the cancellation of the 2002 Mustang Cobra, and the impact of the Terminators.

Ford charged you a fee to be an SVT dealer, and it was several thousand dollars. But included in that fee, they required a sales representative and a service representative to go to training – which was both classroom and hands-on training – to understand the philosophy of the program, what the intent was, and the approach to exclusivity.

Their vision was that when customers came in to buy this kind of vehicle, not only were they performance-oriented people, but they wanted to deal with a sales person who was very knowledgeable about the product that they were selling. It wasn't just going to be another marquee vehicle with higher performance or better handling than our mainline cars – it was supposed to be like a boutique inside the Ford dealer, where the buyer got special treatment and dealt with a very knowledgeable person to make the purchase experience completely different from buying a regular vehicle.

They would also bring the engineers who were designing and developing the cars to the training programs. The programs would run two or three days, so we would have time to sit with them and discuss what they were doing and where they were coming from as a manufacturer. You'd learn some interesting things. Being on the retail side, you didn't really realize what all went into developing and building those products.

When we got word from Ford that the 2002 was cancelled and wasn't going to be produced, the concern that we had was, when you drop a model year, you potentially are going to disrupt the buying schedule of customers. You're also going to undermine their confidence in that product line. Despite that fact, when that '03 car came out, it just totally accelerated SVT demand. It was such a dramatically different car that it just changed the market immensely for SVT. Not only did it bring a number of people in to buy those cars and generate a tremendous amount of traffic and interest in that vehicle, but it generated a tremendous amount of traffic for the dealership in people who bought other products.

In 2004, they loosened up the restriction that you had to be a trained, certified dealer in order to sell the cars. They'd built a lot of Cobras in 2003, and in 2004 they cut that number significantly. Ford was concerned about how well the car would continue to sell. What frustrated us as a dealer was, there we were: we went through all the training, and we had the certified tech that was required to be in the service department. And all of a sudden any dealer could sell and service those cars.

And then came the Shelby GT500. The SVT brand, at that point, had developed a significant amount of value to customers in the industry. Now we've taken that SVT badge and – though the car's built by the same group of people – they turn around and put Shelby's name on it. Ford felt that the Shelby name on the car was going to command more value than SVT. Shelby really didn't have anything to do with it – it was strictly just a marketing aspect of the vehicle.

The SVT market before this still had a little bit older buying group – the muscle car performance guys – but it also appealed to a lot more young people. Now the car's gotten more expensive, now it's got the Shelby name on it which pulls in nostalgia for an older group of people, so the median age and the buyer changed at that point.

If you look at the performance market that's out there today, there's definitely a market of unique buyers for those cars. That plan that Ford had in 2003 with special treatment for those people, and the extensive training for the sales and service people to create that experience for the customer – I think there's definitely room for a boutique business like that inside the dealership today.

But the Terminators? Even today, when we get our hands on one of those cars, we get calls from everywhere from people that are looking for those cars and want to buy them. They're getting few and far between as the days go by, but the demand for them is still there.

When SVT was created, one key aspect was recognition that program approval for the team would be outside of Ford's normal channels. After all, SVT's goal is to create high performance, high profile vehicles built in low volume. By necessity, the focus of SVT would always be on vehicle impact rather than pure profitability.

As such, SVT's streamlined accountability directed the organization to a unique means of gaining program approval. Basically, Tom Scarpello and John Coletti – representing SVT marketing and engineering respectively – had to plead their case before a gathering of "SVT Stakeholders." This group of Ford executives had the final power to approve the business case presented by Scarpello and Coletti, rather than send SVT proposals swimming through a complex chain of command in search of approval.

"The stakeholders tend to go with our recommendations, and I can't remember one time when the stakeholders did not agree with our recommendation in all the years I've been here," Coletti says.

But this time, Coletti's quest for approval of a supercharged Cobra program had very real potential to turn out quite differently. The reason had to do with that most important aspect of the auto business: the bottom line.

Closing the Deals

Selling vehicles developed by Ford's Special Vehicle Team involves far more than just sticking up signs emblazoned with SVT's bold red logo. Just as SVT's cars are the elite automobiles of Ford's product lineup, so too are SVT dealers among the very best of the thousands of Ford dealerships across the US and in Canada.

"Even though we're very small in terms of the overall volume of a company like Ford Motor Company, both in terms of units as well as dollars, we are to some extent very similar to a small car company," explains Bob Lewis. Lewis oversees SVT's relationship with the Ford dealers who sell its vehicles, and also chairs the influential Dealer

Advisory Board, made up of representative SVT dealerships. "We have dealer issues, we have consumer issues, we have engineering issues, we have financial issues and all of those things.

"In the US alone, you're dealing with over 600 dealers. They enroll in our program, they make investments both financial as well as in personnel – training, time out of the dealership, all those sorts of things – and in turn they certainly expect to get something for their investment. You hope that the product you're delivering to them is the quality that the marketplace expects, that has the qualities in terms of performance and drivability and so forth that the market expects. But you know, there is still a business equation that is all part of this, and the dealers will be very happy if the inventory is turning, they're making reasonable profits, and they're getting the supply that they expect to get. Then the dealers are all very happy."

But for the dealers to be happy, they must have cars to sell – and Coletti's proposal to supercharge the new Cobra had a very real impact on this fundamental relationship. There was no way the supercharged Cobra could be developed in time for model year 2002. That meant Coletti's quest for power would cost the dealers a selling season.

"If we come and we decide that we're going to eliminate a year of production, that has an impact on lots of people," Lewis notes. "You may have customers that had orders that were submitted already, you have dealers that have pre-sold some of the inventory, you've got guys that have gone to training – you've got lots of issues that suddenly you've either got to come to terms with or at least explain very clearly why you've arrived at the decision you've arrived at."

But that explanation can only go so far. Under the veil of secrecy surrounding new model development, program specifics are closely guarded secrets. So Lewis couldn't even reveal Coletti's new mandate to his own dealers.

"Rarely are you in a position to say, 'We're going to make it all better, and here's what we have on the drawing board – this is what it is,'" Lewis says. "Unless you're prepared to announce it to the whole world, you don't announce that to the dealers."

In the end, the question was: in the eyes of SVT's decision makers – from Coletti and the engineering team to Scarpello and Lewis in the sales and marketing realm – was more power for the Cobra a good enough reason to scrap the 2002 Cobra?

"If you're a dealer, and you've made a commitment, and you've got an investment that's financial as well as in training and so forth, well, you're expecting the company to deliver the product that you're expecting them to deliver," Lewis says. "Wouldn't you be upset if somebody came out and said, 'This is what we're going to deliver to you, and these are the time frames we're going to do it in,' and then for whatever reason part of it doesn't materialize? They either expect to be compensated or expect you to come out with something where there's a very good reason for why you didn't deliver on that promise you made."

Well aware of Lewis' concerns, but positive that the supercharged Cobra was indeed the "very good reason" that justified waiting until 2003, Coletti and Scarpello pressed on, preparing to face their biggest hurdle – selling to program to the SVT Stakeholders.

Driving the Stake

Facing the stakeholders who would determine the future of the supercharged Cobra, one would think Tom Scarpello and John Coletti would have arrived at the November 2000 meeting armed with an air tight case of solid facts and figures. Instead, what they had were a lot of questions and plenty of vague assumptions. They had no choice – Coletti's decision to go with the supercharger had just been made two months earlier, and the program was in a state that could best be described as fluid.

"We went into our stakeholders group, the group of vice presidents who basically approve all of our car programs, and we told them, 'Here's what we originally set out to do,'" Scarpello remembers. "'We built prototypes, we drove them – we don't think it's good enough. We want to go higher performance. Here's what it's going to take: it's going to take this much time, we're going to lose the '02 model year, it's about this much money, we think we have a handle on the cost but we're not absolutely sure…'"

Adding to the doubt was the fact that early dynamometer engine tests – to prove the capability of the 4.6 liter Mustang engine to act as host to the Eaton supercharger – were not going well. At all.

Above: Being part of SVT's dealer program was a point of pride for Ford dealerships across the country, including Jack Demmer Ford in Michigan. Sadly, by 2004, the exclusivity was diluted by decisions made within Ford's corporate hierarchy.

Photo: Marcie Cipriani

Opposite: Reflecting the high standards of SVT in its glory, the warm letter of welcome sent to new Terminator owners made them feel part of an exclusive club. The membership may have not been cheap, but they saw the exciting benefits every time they looked in the garage.

October 25, 2004

Dear ████

Congratulations on your decision to acquire a new Ford . This very special performance vehicle is designed to provide years of enjoyment. We sincerely appreciate your choice of an SVT product.

The Ford Special Vehicle Team is a dedicated group of automobile enthusiasts who are responsible for the development and marketing of limited-edition, high-performance vehicles for Ford Motor Company. Ford created SVT in 1991, with a simple but ambitious mission:

• Create a line of high-performance Ford vehicles that satisfy demanding enthusiasts
• Back-up those products with a group of dedicated Ford dealers who understand the performance customer

During the past decade, SVT has enjoyed considerable success in the performance marketplace. Our products have graced the covers of the world's best-known automotive magazines, and have been adopted by the most discriminating driving enthusiasts. But SVT is about more than great cars and trucks; it's really about a philosophy. From design to engineering, manufacturing to marketing, all the way to the service departments at SVT dealerships, SVT strives to do things better. And part of the commitment to doing things better is offering unique, personalized services to enhance the ownership experience, such as:

• **SVT Premium Service:** Owners and lessees of eligible model year SVT vehicles will be provided with a complimentary loaner vehicle when their SVT vehicle is in for service (includes warranty work and routine maintenance, other than oil changes). The dealership will also wash and vacuum the vehicle, unless requested otherwise.

• **SVT Owners Association One-Year Membership:** The SVT Owners Association is a club designed to enhance the experience of owning an SVT vehicle through events and learning activities, as well as the camaraderie of spending time with other SVT enthusiasts. Your new vehicle purchase or lease entitles you to a <u>free</u> one-year membership. Membership materials are enclosed.

• **Team Ford Racing One-Year Membership:** Team Ford Racing provides inside access to news about Ford Racing teams and drivers, exclusive race-day hospitality programs, access to test sessions, and other benefits. You will be automatically enrolled for a free one-year membership.

• **Certificate of Authenticity:** In recognition of your vehicle's exclusivity, the certificate documents your vehicle's date of production, vehicle identification number, final assembly plant, and production sequence number. Certificates are printed 60 to 90 days after production is complete, and will be mailed to you automatically.

• **SVT Info Center:** Have a question or want information about your SVT vehicle, or any of our new products? Just call the SVT Info Center at 800-FORD-SVT. We will handle your request or get you in touch with someone who can.

• **SVT Website:** The official SVT site, <u>www.svt.ford.com</u>, will provide you with frequently updated information on products, events and many other areas of interest for SVT owners.

We hope you take full advantage of all the benefits of SVT ownership, so that you can experience the same passion for excellence that guides us in everything we do.

Thanks again for your support!

John Coletti
Director of SVT Programs
Ford Special Vehicle Team

Tom Scarpello
Marketing and Sales Manager
Ford Special Vehicle Team

"The guys put together the first supercharged engines and we were starting to test them to see how far we could go," Coletti says. "Could we deliver? Well, we were blowing up engines right and left in that dyno cell.

"I still remember walking in there (to the stakeholder meeting) and saying, 'Well, gentlemen, we recommend this program. However, I want you to know we have not had one successful dynamometer pass yet.' The engines weren't even getting to ten or twelve hours before we were blowing them up."

Unhappy dealers? An engine that couldn't even pass a dyno test? Not to mention a suspension that had to be redesigned to support the weight of

Ford CEO Bill Ford is seen celebrating the 300 millionth vehicle built by the company, a Mustang that rolled off the line at Dearborn Assembly Plant in November 2003.
Photo: Ford Motor Company

that engine? The Cobra program was one that looked to be skating the thin edge between success and failure – and definitely leaning toward the latter. Just how much faith did the stakeholders have in SVT?

Enough to listen to the one compelling argument that Coletti and Scarpello could present.

"We know that this is the right thing to do to the car," Scarpello remembers telling the gathering. "And how do we know it? Well, we haven't done all these market studies, and we don't have all kinds of research and have all kinds of data – but we know it because we work in this market segment. We understand the customer, and we think it's the right thing to do."

Bill Ford had come to appreciate the determination shown by Coletti's vision and Scarpello's support.

"The automobile industry is a very competitive, numbers-driven business," Ford notes. "We have to make a profit to stay in business. But if you just let the numbers drive all of your decisions, you won't be in business very long. That's why you need people who have good instincts and strong convictions. And it's interesting – the true believers are usually the ones who find a way to make the numbers work, even after everyone else has given up."

At the stakeholder meeting, Bob Rewey, a member of the board as a Ford group vice president, confronted Coletti with the obvious question. "'John, you're telling me you don't have an engine that can live, and you want me to approve the program?' I remember his reaction was like this," Coletti laughs, imitating a look of complete disbelief. "He's sitting there like that, he asked me that question. Then he goes, 'Well, OK, if you want it. If you guys think you can go for it – do it.'"

"When that happened, everybody got so charged up," Scarpello says. "It was like a huge vote of confidence in our team from management. The Cobra is the flagship of SVT, and to have that back in our organizational area for development was the right thing to do and we felt good about that."

And unlike the modest 2002 Cobra that had been agreed upon as a compromise, SVT could now create a supercharged beast that would stand as a shining example of modern muscle – the revolutionary change the team had longed to implement.

"We wanted to show the whole world what we can do," Scarpello admits. "So when we got the approval to go with the supercharged engine, it made us say, 'This is the car that we want to build and we are being given the chance to really do it the way we want to do it.' So it was even more motivating."

Additional motivation would come in the form of the program's code name. During an early meeting that included Primo Goffi and the man who would ultimately be responsible for the success or failure of the 2003 Cobra, program manager Tom Bochenek, the question of what to call the project arose.

"The Focus and the '03 Cobra were concurrent, and they were the first SVT programs that had code names," notes Goffi. "There were some names thrown out that were kind of soft, and a couple of other guys

Tom Bochenek (left) was charged by John Coletti with bringing the supercharged Cobra to life, a project given the "Terminator" code name by Primo Goffi (right).
Photo: Frank Moriarty

threw out a couple of other things. But we said, 'No, we can't have anything like that – it's gotta be something that signifies it's just going to kill everything!' And I'm pretty sure (SVT engineer) Dave Dempster said something like 'Commando' or something like that – and I said, 'Naw, it's gotta be something stronger than that. How about Terminator?' And it was, 'Oh – OK!' And it kind of stuck."

"It was nice and bold, just a stomper," Bochenek laughs.

But a catchy program name was the least of SVT's problems. The new Cobra had to be ready for a Spring, 2002 introduction as a 2003 model. In a world where new automotive product development almost always takes years, SVT had just eighteen months to build their Terminator. Already, the clock was relentlessly ticking.

"Once we decide to do this, we're doing this," is Bochenek's recollection of the team attitude. "When we're in the team there is no doubt. I happened to look through some of my minutes from one of the meetings we had after the Western Drive. It was broken down 'Vehicle,' 'Chassis,' 'Powertrain,' but the first line item? It says, 'Terminator or bust!' There was no turning back."

CHAPTER 3 APPEARANCES COUNT

Success by Design

"The law of costs and competition does not take artists into account."

That quote is attributed to Pinin Farina in the book *Pininfarina: Art and Industry 1930-2000*, an account of the influential Italian design concern that has been responsible for some of the automotive world's most dramatic designs. A young Pinin, first testing the waters of the automotive industry, had quickly come to the sobering conclusion that the art of auto design must coexist with the realities of mass production.

That this sentiment might resonate with Camilo Pardo would come as no surprise. After all, Pardo is an accomplished artist, sculptor, clothing and furniture stylist – and one of Ford Motor Company's brightest and most talented automotive designers.

Pardo joined Ford shortly after his graduation in 1985 from the Center for Creative Studies in Detroit, and worked in Ford's domestic Advance Design studio before moving on to the company's European studios. Returning to Ford's headquarters in Dearborn, Michigan, Camilo received a challenging new assignment in 1999 – design manager for SVT.

"SVT brings in a lot of interest and gets a lot of coverage and does the company a lot of good because it's always in the limelight. It creates all this interest and excitement because of its great products," Pardo says of working for the team. But from a design perspective, there are always forces that must be balanced when working within the realm of SVT.

"There are certain things that design wants and certain things that they want from engineering and it's a real fight to meet halfway," Pardo confirms. "Everybody has expectations, and everybody has a vision. Marketing has a vision, John Coletti has a vision, and we listen and we put together an artistic vision of what the vehicle should be."

Overseeing SVT designs meant Pardo's domain included the team's Focus and F-150 Lightning projects, but there were two vehicles that were closest to his heart: the Cobra, and Petunia.

Camilo Pardo became an automotive design star at Ford Motor Company. Although he came to utilize information technology in his efforts, Pardo was hands-on in his design for the Ford GT supercar – a project that influenced Camilo's thoughts for the Terminator.
Photo: Ford Motor Company

Petunia? Like the supercharged Cobra and its "Terminator" development moniker, there was another code-named special vehicle under development by SVT concurrently with the Cobra. Though the program was given the most bland title possible, Petunia was in every way as dramatic as the Cobra – for in reality it denoted the Ford GT, the bold reworking of the company's amazing GT40 program of the late 1960s.

It was Pardo's vision that shaped the thrilling, modern interpretation of a high performance classic that is the GT – and the Terminator benefited from both Camilo's touch and from the fact that it was designed alongside the in-progress supercar, at a remote off-site design studio beginning in mid-2000.

"We were in a very nice location that was kind of secluded, outside of a lot of traffic," Pardo notes of the site, with access restricted to studio personnel only. "There weren't 100 opinions walking through."

In a state of relative creative isolation, Pardo considered the design heritage of the Cobra.

"What you start with is to look at the history of it," Camilo explains. "You make sure you understand what all the Cobras have looked like on this body, and where it's progressed from. So you line them all up – and now you understand where you're coming from, and you get a feel for where you're going. It's always good to keep echoing, so you have a nice progression and there's a relationship, a visual relationship. So if somebody sees it, they say, 'Oh, that's a Cobra.'"

But with such a heritage comes a binding set of constraints.

"When you start with a vehicle like the Mustang, you've got a lot of restrictions," Pardo notes. "Fortunately, we could do a hood, fender, the whole fascia and rear fascia, and we wanted the deck lid – but you already have certain parameters that hold you pretty tight. So the variations don't get as dramatic as something like the Ford GT."

Still, the Cobra program benefited from its proximity to the GT project, as Camilo focused his attention on both of the vehicles. He took advantage of

Camilo Pardo was given the responsibility of developing the character of SVT's high-profile vehicles.
Photo: Frank Moriarity

the opportunity to share themes between these autos that would soon carry Ford's performance banner on the streets.

"We had the Ford GT in development at the time, and we were trying to come up with some themes and some ideas. On paper, it's a lot easier to generate ideas. There's a lot of flexibility there – you can make water look like it flows up hill," Camilo laughs. "But when you get down to your parameters – saving the quarterpanels, the existing quarterpanels and things like that – everything becomes reality.

"It put restrictions on the form development and your integration from one surface to another, wherever there was a cut line," Pardo continues. "So, when we had the two cars there, one of our directors came in and said, 'Why don't you do to the Cobra what you're doing to the GT?' And it made some sense to get some family in the vehicle there. 'Let's put extractors on the hood instead of air intakes,' so that's where that came from. That's Ford GT-influenced. 'Let's put some running lamps down there,' so we put the running lamps in there, plus the brake cooling intakes. So they were all the little bits of GT DNA going into the car."

Though Pardo was, by necessity, unable to start from the proverbial blank piece of paper, he immediately knew there were major improvements to be made, and communicated that fact to J Mays, leader of Ford's design group.

"When I saw the previous Cobra, and I saw the way it looked, I told our director that it shouldn't be a problem to make an improvement," Pardo states.

"One of the definite goals with the Cobra was to simplify and fix the approach angle distortion, what I call a distortion in the previous Cobra," he says. "Because the corners of the vehicle were a lot higher than the center of the air dam, the air dam had a negative crown. And that always looked like a plastics problem to me. We wanted to correct that desperately."

That approach springs from Pardo's philosophy of design: "I want things to be very mature, but at the same time I want things to be very aggressive." Camilo relied on his extensive studies of high performance designs, applying subtle use of spatial relationships to "tailor" the Cobra.

The Ford GT supercar (top) was designed at the same time as the Terminator (bottom), both in complete secrecy. Obviously visual cues from one pollinated the other, with Camilo Pardo cleverly envisioning a shared design heritage for Ford's most elite vehicles.
Photos: Ford Motor Company, Marcie Cipriani

"I wanted something that basically had a really nice relationship to the ground, and that would be parallel," Pardo explains. "When you start undulating a lot, the vehicle starts divorcing itself from the ground. This thing, I really wanted it to look like it was stable, and in order – orderly, mature, and organized. That was pretty much what we were going for in the geometry of all the components like the air intakes, the driving lamps, the brake intakes, and the geometry also of the hood."

Indeed, it's in the subtle tuning of aspects like the hood that Pardo's art expresses itself in ways that simply make the car look "right."

"I'm very particular about wheels. It's something where you have to keep a really clear mind when you're doing them."

"I don't know how many people really appreciate it unless you drive one Mustang Cobra up to the other of the previous year," he says, "but on the hood in the previous vehicle, there is a break above the headlamps. And we just took that and cleaned it into one sweep. So you have one sweep above the lamps, and one sweep on the bottom on the ground, so now the lines of car are really working together.

"That's what is the interesting thing about this car," Pardo insists. "It's organized, with the ground. It's related to the ground, kind of like a stock car. And the hood is cleaned up, and all the lines relate in a view all the way down."

This concept of simplicity played a crucial role in other aspects of the Terminator's design.

"We caught a little grief for these wheels because they're a little too simple," Pardo says of the understated, five-spoke design selected for the new Cobra. "But we like simple wheels – simple wheels that look large and clean, not busy. I'm very particular about wheels. It's something where you have to keep a really clear mind when you're doing them. Some people get overexcited when they do wheels, and they get really busy, and it becomes an eyesore."

Acting as the intermediary between this fluid, emotional realm of automotive art and the hard and fast world of engineering rules was Celeste Kupczewski, on her first assignment for John Coletti and Cobra program manager Tom Bochenek. Kupczewski had joined SVT at the time that Pardo was just beginning his Cobra design labors. Her job was to shepherd Camilo's visions from concepts to practical reality, all in pursuit of making the new Cobra something special.

"Basically, engineering is a support function to the studio design," Kupczewski explains, "so it was my responsibility to work with Camilo and make sure that the designs that he was coming up with were feasible for manufacturing."

Traditionally, relationships between styling and engineering can be contentious at best. While the SVT engineers and Pardo's team interfaced well – with communication enhanced greatly by Kupczewski's efforts – some SVT members of the technical persuasion can't resist referring to the denizens of the design studio as "The Men in Black."

Early vehicle renderings hint at the final product design.
Photos: Ford Motor Company

Putting the Pieces Together

Though Camilo Pardo was armed with a host of ideas in mind and a growing pile of sketches and drawings, it's notoriously difficult to assess design subtleties without seeing them full scale. Pardo and Kupczewski began to migrate the designer's concepts from paper to reality.

The optimal method for such full scale analysis would have been to utilize one of Ford's Mustang clay armatures – basically, a full-scale Mustang entity that hosts design modeling clay. This clay can then be molded into the shape of any planned design enhancement on the armature. There was just one problem.

"Here's an excellent example of SVT's 'think outside of the box' mentality," Kupczewski relates. "We were under the gun for timing, but we couldn't get one of the Mustang clay armatures because they were busy doing their mainstream programs. So we couldn't get a clay. And it was, what do we do? What can we do to make this happen? Well, Camilo and the studio said, 'Well, just get us a car. We'll make it happen.' We worked on a real vehicle and took the hood off, took the fascias off, and threw clay on it."

"We actually did it on a real Mustang, which is a real pain in the butt because that thing has a lot of tolerances, so it moves and it's hard to predict," Pardo notes. "If you have a full clay you have a stable surface that's at its optimum. And that's also a problem, because you're designing for an optimum and that's not what's going to completely come out of the assembly line. But that's how we work with it. We build an armature, we work with math data, we have math modelers, we have a mill that will mill out the information that we developed. Or we can develop surfaces from sculpting it, just free sculpting it with the modelers trying to get the right solution by feel, the traditional way. The historical method! Which is always, always necessary at one stage of every program."

"So that's how we worked that one up," Pardo concludes. "All of the new parts were modeled in clay against metal parts, and I don't think we cast them – we went right to math and sent them off to be tooled up."

But the use of clay appended to an actual metal vehicle in this phase did lead to some early problems with those tooled components. The issues arose during the Confirmation Prototype builds, when the assemblies are actually tested.

"When we went through CP, the hoods and the fascias had been designed flush on the clay," Kupczewski explains. "We were driving cars off the end of the line that you could throw a football through the gap between the hood and the fascia, just because of the build tolerances and the way the clay was scanned off of a real vehicle. It was those types of things that made ourselves a little more work than we might have had if we had the normal process. But we got the job done – we met the timing, we dealt with it in the tooling. We had to do some tooling changes, and it cost us a couple of dollars at the end of the program, but ultimately I think it was a great example of, we really don't have the right tools to do this but how are we going to do it anyway?"

Celeste Kupczewski was charged with making sure the designs created by Camilo Pardo would fit into the program's financial and engineering constraints.
Photo: Frank Moriarity

As the new Cobra began to take its three-dimensional shape, the importance of Kupczewski's job became ever more apparent. Pardo's creativity might yield a bounty of exciting design aspects, but it was up to Celeste to find out if they could really be done.

"Engineering would come in and say, 'Well, I don't have any feasible way of manufacturing that on a large scale,'" Kupczewski says of reactions to certain aspects of Pardo's design. "You know, there are always things you can do, but piece pricing and the investment in tooling is always a huge constraint on the program. So we need to come up with the lowest cost way to manufacture something, and that would drive Camilo's constraints as far as how radical he could go with the design.

"So, we're primarily a support function and we keep our eyes on the feasibility," Celeste continues. "I had fourteen full service suppliers underneath me, and I would bring in to the studio the actual people that design and manufacture the hard parts and kind of be the liaison between the studio and the suppliers and keep the information flow going. I was primarily the communication gateway between what Camilo wanted to do and what's actually capable and feasible in hard tooling."

Perfect examples of this process were Camilo's desire for 18-inch wheels – vetoed due to wheel well clearance issues – and his idea for a new Cobra spoiler.

"I wish we could have done more with the spoiler," Pardo laments. "The spoiler I would have liked to have more of a NASCAR-like blade, just standing up. But it was hard for them to produce that."

Though Camilo's blade spoiler did not make it past the design phase, simple enhancements like vertical rocker panels and an uncomplicated-yet-menacing redesign of the Cobra's front end did strikingly improve the appearance of the production Terminator, following Pardo's "control of geometry" mantra.

"I thought that that's what this thing needed – it needed a clean up," Pardo says of the Cobra's design status before the Terminator. "I thought that the one before this was just getting a little out of control, so it needed a cleanup. It needed a good foundation. And once you have a good foundation, you can build up from that – just make sure it's all integrated and tailored right. Because this hot rod thing gets out of control – it's just stuff stuck on stuff and cladding and busy wheels…

"It's like it's your kids," Pardo illustrates. "You've got to make sure that you're feeding them the right food. Because if you don't, they'll just go eat any garbage. And it's the same thing! People just go out and buy it, just because it's for sale. So it's up to us to control it."

Still, Pardo is well aware it's a partnership between the studio and engineering that yields a great automobile.

"They're the guys that know what to do with the engine and how to make it handle, so that's what they do, and they should do it right and do it well. And we go to school to learn about form, function, balance, rhythm, and control, and how to tune a shape – we should deliver that. So, between the two, if you get both of them nice and in good control, then you'll have a very nice product."

Light in the Tunnel

Throughout the summer of 2000 Camilo Pardo had made great progress in improving the iconic Mustang's appearance. Interestingly, Pardo felt his efforts paid greatest dividends when applied to Cobra coupes, to the extent that lighter colors were most effective in communicating design subtleties.

"Actually, the vehicle that I really like the most is the hardtop," Camilo reveals. "I have a real hard time with convertibles, they look like… A lot of times when you take a coupe and you cut it, the coupes rely on the unity of the C pillar and roof to complete the full composition. And when you cut coupes, you just sometimes disconnect the flow of the shape.

"The coupe is beautiful composition – but is it (the model) better as a coupe or better as a convertible? It's more fun as a convertible, and the basic perception of all things just by the mentality is, 'Oh it's great to have a convertible, it's better!' But are people really looking? This looks better as a coupe."

Turning to the color palette, Camilo explains, "I usually like dark colored cars – the black color helps hide all the things I don't want to look at. But I was so confident with the graphics that we laid out that you can see the graphics in a silver, or white, or yellow car. With a car that you are confident about the design, and the shape of the glass, the shape of the openings – you can go white! You can see the design of it."

The validity of Camilo's sense of design was proven in August, 2000, when a special market research event was held at the SVT facility. The Mustang bearing Pardo's clayed enhancements was dressed in Dynoc, a material that made the car appear as though it was finished and painted. It was then presented to a small, select group of SVT Owners Association members, who were told they were seeing a concept car for a future Mustang program. In reality, they were seeing the fully-approved design theme of the new Cobra. The hybrid clay/real vehicle was unveiled to an overwhelmingly enthusiastic reaction.

But then came September – and the sudden impact of John Coletti's Western Drive displeasure. The 2002 Cobra was now a 2003 Cobra – and the newly-supercharged engine of the Terminator would be considerably taller than the dimensions of the original design. The supercharger also required greater cooling. Unavoidably, Camilo's enhancements were facing practical revisions under the gun – so the Terminator made its first journey, albeit via shipping.

"That's the point when we ended up buying some time in the wind tunnel at Lockheed Martin in Atlanta," Kupczewski explains. "We brought the clay vehicle down there, and we were trying to get as much downforce out of the vehicle as we could. And we were also trying to optimize the engine package cooling, because we knew when we went with the supercharger that we were going to have some cooling issues on the vehicle.

"So we needed to maximize the air openings in the front fascia, and we also wanted to get some of the heat out of the engine compartment," Kupczewski continues. "So there was more work on the hood scoops. We brought them into the wind tunnel to optimize the position within the hood of where the air stream was that would push the most air out."

"I can remember there was quite a bit of a struggle. I think we went up to go down," laughs Camilo. But raising the center of the hood to accommodate the Eaton supercharger was a real concern. "We had to go up in the center so we could take the extractors down on the sides. But all the other Cobras had air intakes, so it was nice to do extractors, real deep, different extractors."

The hood extractor scoops journeyed from the very front of the hood – where Pardo had initially placed them – farther back toward the rear edge, eventually migrating to their production location just under eighteen inches from the hood's leading edge. While in the wind tunnel, the Terminator's spoiler height was also finalized. Though quite different from Pardo's vision of a NASCAR blade spoiler, the final design was elevated by another inch at Lockheed Martin to increase downforce, ensuring its presence was recognizable by the high-speed air flow.

Further slight alterations came when the suppliers who build the actual production parts reviewed Pardo's work.

"There's four or five months when we're in the studio doing the tweaking," Kupczewski says, "and you start to bring the full service suppliers in to do their tooling feasibility. 'Well, we can't make that radius and we need to soften it' – that's always like pulling teeth because those crisp lines are part of the design theme."

Like most designers, Camilo Pardo would have happily used more time to tweak and refine his design. But now the Terminator was scheduled to debut early in 2002 as a 2003 model – there was no more time for the designer's art.

"I was always in there yelling at him, that we needed to keep moving," Kupczewski admits. "We realize that it's hard, when you go into a creative process – there's always that next thing you could do, or how much further can we take this, or let's think about this a little bit longer and make it better. But unfortunately – especially with the change between the naturally aspirated engine and the supercharger – we were under some really heavy constraints.

"This was by far the fastest that we've ever gone through a clay process all the way to an appearance approval and surface release," Celeste continues. "It was unbelievable that we managed to do that entire process with the pressure that Camilo was under in six months. The communication, I think we worked really well. We all had access to the studio, and like Camilo said, you didn't have all those other opinions – we were the only ones in there. I was there every day, and that was my sole focus: whenever Camilo or any of the studio engineers needed something, they called me, and I was there right away to get it resolved. I think we worked really well together, and being a small team, that really helps a lot, not having all the different filters to go through. It was pretty much just me and Camilo making everything happen and we were able to go really fast that way."

For Pardo, the hectic birth of the Terminator's design was well worth the effort, and the fact that it was created alongside the GT only adds to his fondness for that period of time.

"It was great," Camilo enthuses. "It was working on the Mustang that'll come out with more horsepower than any Mustang's ever had on the street, and on this Ford GT that's just going to be a world-class sports car. So it was just the two best projects that you could have for Ford if you like high performance…

"There's a lot that goes into these things, and sometimes the cars that are already established make it even more difficult and challenging," Pardo concludes. "This was quite challenging to get through because of the layout and the stakes in the ground that were already there with the platform that you're working with. I would have liked to really make some changes on it, but I'm never really completely satisfied. But that's what keeps us striving to get better."

In the end, how does Pardo sum up his work on the Terminator project? "Running around hard and crazy," he laughs. "But everything we were doing was just about the fastest vehicles in the company. I couldn't have it better than that; that's exactly what I wanted."

LSW T 1655   RUN 20
02 MUSTANG
COBER

LSW T 1655   RUN 20
02 MUSTANG
COBER

LSW T 1655   RUN 24
02 MUSTANG
COBER

1655   RUN 39
MUSTANG
BRA

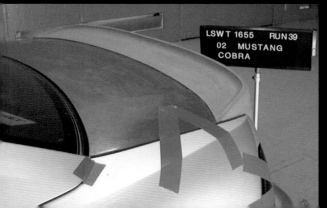

LSW T 1655   RUN 39
02 MUSTANG
COBRA

LSW T 1655   RUN 40
02 MUSTANG
COBRA

LSW T 1655   RUN 43
02 MUSTANG
COBRA

To ensure Camilo Pardo's design was not only stylish but aerodynamically efficient, wind tunnel tests took place at the Lockheed Martin facility in Atlanta, GA.

Photos courtesy Celeste Kupczewski

CHAPTER 4 HANDLING WITH CARE

Dynamic Reaction

As the end of the year 2000 loomed, there were two things that were certain about SVT's Terminator program: what the car would look like, and that it would have a supercharged engine. But while Camilo Pardo had things under control as far as the new Cobra's appearance, every other aspect of Terminator development was in a state of barely controlled chaos.

"The downstream effects of putting in a powerplant such as that – when we went to supercharging – that created a domino effect, or a ripple through the system, where all of the other downstream components have to be sized accordingly," says Cobra team manager Primo Goffi. "It ended up causing a new driveshaft, structural supports for the differential, half shafts, all the way to the wheels."

Terminator program manager Tom Bochenek adds, "You've got the engine, you've got the supercharger, you've got an all new air plenum, clutch, induction system, all new radiator, coolers, intercooler, power steering cooler…"

The list must have seemed endless, but there was no time to worry about workloads – the program deadline was just over a year away. Unlike

typical years-long development efforts, the Terminator was due to hit the streets in a matter of months, early in 2002.

"We wanted to minimize the amount of time that we were out of the market, because we didn't have a 2000 car, we had an '01 car, we wouldn't have an '02 car – the longer you stayed out of the market, that was an issue," Goffi states. "We wanted to be in the market for the spring buying season with the car – from a marketing and sales standpoint I think that was an important aspect of it. If we delayed any longer…"

No one in SVT wanted to think about what would happen if they missed that deadline, having already cancelled the 2002 model. The result was that every functional aspect of the Cobra was under revision at the same time.

"You've got to get a baseline and start to build some prototype vehicles and put the best you know in those cars and keep going," Bochenek says. "But everything's got to go on in parallel – there's no serial process. You've got your little hiccups as you go, but you've got to recover. To be quite honest, the body stuff was further along than anything because we had started earlier with the naturally aspirated version. So we were really waiting for everything else to catch up to the body."

One area that had a long way to go before reaching near-completion status was the Terminator's handling package. The decision to supercharge had delivered a real blow to Tom Chapman's vehicle dynamics and chassis systems team. The problem was one of weight: the supercharged 4.6-liter engine would be substantially heavier than the naturally aspirated version. Simply put, the chassis tuning applied by the team to the 2002 Cobra might as well be thrown out the window.

"We kind of fell off our chairs," engineer Enzo Campagnolo says of the supercharger decree. "We've got a lot more work to do from a chassis standpoint because a significant amount of weight was added to the front end. And we already basically had a tuning we were working on for what the normally aspirated car was going to be, and now that didn't work at all."

"We were about 80% complete with all of the ride and handling and had some really great improvements planned that eventually had to be cut because of cost reasons once the new engine came up," reveals Mark Dipko, SVT's lead chassis engineer on the Cobra program. "At the time it had all new brakes, steering, 18-inch wheels, a new differential, and a bunch of other unique parts… When the supercharger came in, the whole strategy changed – and we basically had to start chassis development at ground zero."

Tom Chapman, Jeff Grauer and Enzo Campagnolo (left to right) were all involved in tuning the handling characteristics of the Terminator.
Photo: Frank Moriarity

concepts and rough components. "Before the engines were available, we bolted 100 pounds of lead bars into the front of two Cobras, one coupe and one convertible. This allowed me to concentrate on the fore/aft balance of the car and get springs and shocks and some fundamental balance of the car. This gave us a great head start since the engines were arriving so late."

"Obviously, the two biggest masses in the vehicle system are the body itself and the powertrain," points out chassis systems supervisor Tom Chapman. "So it's not just total mass that you have to deal with, it's center of gravity height. You can't just tape shot bags onto the hood – you'll get the right axle weight but the CG's too high. So we came up with approximate locations to put ballast. We had big chunks of lead, and we'd bore holes and screw them to the fender aprons."

Manufacturing manager at Dearborn Assembly Plant, Tom Nichols (left), and SVT's Tom Scarpello discuss the 2000 Cobra R. This factory-built racing machine provided inspiration for the Terminator handling package.
Photo: Ford Motor Company

But there was a vexing impediment that threatened to prevent the revised chassis program from even starting. Until the engine development reached a stage where the supercharged engine could be provided to the vehicle dynamics team, there was no Terminator engine. And with no engine, there was no way to develop the car's handling characteristics.

Dipko, who had co-developed the race-ready chassis of the 2000 Cobra R with fellow engineer Dean Martin, had no choice but to improvise an ingenious solution to the powerplant dilemma.

"The basic structure of the car was the same, so we simply used 2001 Cobras as our base car and then bolted the new parts onto it for testing," Dipko explains of the Workhorse Prototype level vehicles, hosts to new

Improvising further, lead was even screwed onto the naturally aspirated engine, all in an attempt to get a handle on the parameters thrown askew by the proposed Terminator powerplant.

"You pretty much start looking at everything again," says Enzo Campagnolo. "Really, we looked at geometry, we looked at springs, bars, dampers, the roll balance… We actually made changes to the rear suspension geometry after we had all of the right parts in the car, and found it to be a significant improvement. We revised the rear roll steer, just to compensate for some of the other factors that were working against us. We actually retuned all of the bushings on the car as well, just to get it be as balanced as we possibly could given the difference in weight."

"Bushings were another big improvement," Mark Dipko agrees. "We used much firmer bushings for the IRS and to help control deflection under

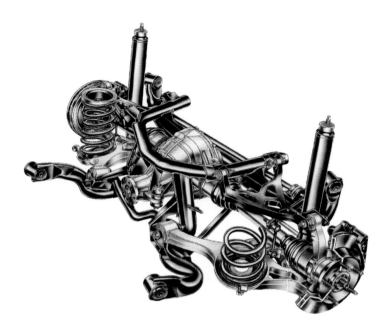

acceleration and hard cornering – resulting in much better predictability and control, with only a slight increase in harshness. I also used the bushings to help tune the compliance steer effects which helped give the car its progressive handling characteristics."

Obviously, handling is crucial to a vehicle's success, and every design presents its challenges. But the Terminator presented unique obstacles. With the heavy supercharged engine lurking under the hood, the new Cobra had a weight imbalance from front to rear of 57 to 43 percent – far from an ideal set of circumstances.

"Handling is tricky because of the weight transfer," Dipko readily concedes. "Under braking, the front tires are loaded very heavily and the car wants to understeer, but once you get into the throttle the weight shift can easily overload the rear tires and cause oversteer."

The scale of revisions was intimidating.

"We had changes on the IRS to improve handling and steering feel, an all-new tire program, a new philosophy on springs and bars," Tom Chapman lists.

"And we went from twin tube damper technology to the Bilstein monotubes," Chapman says of a dramatic revision to the vehicle shock absorber strategy. The Bilstein high performance shocks evolved directly from that company's extensive racing success, and the Terminator's monotube gas shocks feature larger piston diameters, improved heat dissipation, and lighter weight.

With a smile, Chapman sums things up: "A lot of work to do."

Above: The Terminator's Independent Rear Suspension was a tremendous advantage when it came to high-speed cornering and overall performance. It would not be until the 2015 model year that the IRS was adapted across the entire Mustang platform – yet another example of the Terminator being ahead of its time. Right: A comparison of the independent rear suspension on the Terminator (left) and the standard suspension on the Mustang GT.
Photos: Marcie Cipriani

Rubber on the Road

Armed with the improvised Workhorse Prototypes that Mark Dipko, Tom Chapman, and the vehicle dynamics team hoped were an adequate simulation of the Terminators-to-be, attention turned to on-track testing.

"We bring one out as soon as we can," Chapman says of the initial runs of test vehicles. "As soon as we can get a prototype built, or reference vehicles for benchmarking, we come out as soon as we possibly can to start getting ourselves dialed in to what it is we need – and we don't leave the track until engineering sign off."

Appearances can be deceptive – these older Cobras bear Terminator components beneath the skin during this test at Road Atlanta in March, 2001.
Photos courtesy Mike Luzader

These early efforts at sites like Ford's Dearborn Proving Grounds Handling Course helped the team develop the personality of the Terminator.

"We ask, how are we going to position the car's image in terms of the Cobra R and everything else, from a chassis dynamics standpoint?" says Campagnolo. "And I think we came to the conclusion that, in terms of spring rates and dampings and whatnot for the coupe, for vehicle dynamics it would be positioned between the existing Cobra and the 2000 Cobra R. So this would split the difference in terms of how the car would behave."

The physical structure of the Terminator coupe allowed Dipko to develop a more aggressive handling approach; softer springs and dampers were dictated by the convertible, which is tuned by design to deliver a more refined ride quality. The coupe's spring rates are 600 lb./in. at all four corners compared to 500 front and 470 rear on the 2001 Cobra; the topless Terminator rides with the 500/470 rates of the 2001 edition coupe. In the end, the convertible's 3780 pound curb weight topped the coupe by 115 pounds.

The Terminator also features an additional tubular cross-brace for the independent rear suspension which, combined with the bushings, handles the increased load brought on by higher performance levels.

There were, however, aspects of the program that the team wish could have been further enhanced. Among these is the steering responsiveness.

"We wish we could have done more," Campagnolo admits. "We had a steering gear that we thought actually provided better feel, but as we worked with the supplier it basically came down to the fact that we were such a low-volume program that they wouldn't supply it to us. And really, the only option that we were left with was to use the carryover gear, which is common with the GT. But given the fact that we had to use that, we did make a couple of changes to the steering rack bushings – we made them stiffer to provide a better feel. Also, to help the steering on-center precision, this car has a unique intermediate shaft that connects the steering wheel down to the steering gear, which is a special low-lash design."

Not surprisingly, attention was also focused on one of the most crucial aspects of vehicle dynamics: tires.

"We treat the tire as a tunable component," Tom Chapman states. "The tire is probably the single most influential component on the whole car. I mean, you can destroy an otherwise fine car with a lousy set of tires. So we take advantage of the tunability of the tires.

"There are literally dozens of different components in a tire that are tunable, and we work with most of those to get the thing dialed right in to our needs," he continues. "You know, a lot of people think that the first thing you do when you buy a new car is get those junk original equipment tires off; that's the biggest mistake you could ever make. The best tires that car's ever going to see – any car, not just Fords – the best tires that a car's ever going to see are the ones that come out of the factory."

"Usually what we do is we look at our loads – what the car weighs to start with, what it's max loads are going to be – and then we in SVT usually wedge the biggest tire that can fit in the front and rear," explains chassis engineer Jeff Grauer. "And then we usually cheat it a little bit from there and go a little bit bigger. You know, make new inner fender linings or whatever it takes. First we have to carry the load, so we have to get a big enough tire to carry the loads, because our cars are usually heavier with bigger engines or superchargers or whatever. And that's where we start with our tire size – go to the tire manufacturers and say, 'OK, we need this size.' Usually, it's the biggest thing that will wedge in…"

Although full testing of actual tire compounds was forced into delay status while awaiting completion of Terminator engine development, the groundwork was well underway to hit the test tracks at full speed as soon as the real engines were available.

"It's pretty typical for all of our programs – and actually most cars within Ford – that you start out with a tire target letter that we issue," says Enzo Campagnolo. "We know what we want to see in the tire in terms of dry traction, wet traction, rolling resistance, tread wear, and on and on and on. So we've got a pretty good idea of what we want. Then we go out to the tire companies and say, 'These are our requirements.'"

The chassis group had done all it could to this point in dealing with the sudden changes spurred by John Coletti's reaction to the 2002 Cobra on the Western Drive months earlier.

"If I would have known we were going to get that monster engine, I could have saved a lot of time in the early stages of development chasing things that would later be eliminated from the program," Mark Dipko assesses. "You are always fighting time – you never feel like you are completely done because there is no perfect tuning, but the more time you have the closer you can get to it."

Burnouts may not be a formal aspect of vehicle dynamics tuning, but that doesn't stop Tom Chapman from lighting up the tires.
Photos courtesy Mike Luzader

Or, as Tom Chapman is quick to note, "A good development engineer is never done."

But for the Terminator, "done" status would have to wait until the powertrain team had resolved an increasingly complex series of obstacles that were plaguing the heavily revised engine. Things were not going well on the dynamometers.

CHAPTER 5 HEART AND SOUL

**Opposite:
2004 Cobra
in Screaming
Yellow.**
*Photo: Marcie
Cipriani*
**Above: Brian
Roback (left)
and Dave
Dempster
(right) had
to find a way
to combine
brute force and
durability for
the Terminator.**
*Photo: Frank
Moriarty*

Ramping up the Power

In the early 1990s, the great Dale Earnhardt had yet to win a Daytona 500, the race he coveted victory in the most. According to legend, late one New Year's Eve his brilliant engine builder, James "Spenny" Clendenen, was pushing a Chevrolet race engine on a dynamometer for all it was worth, in the hopes of helping Earnhardt finally make his way to victory lane in the 500. But as often happens when engines are stressed far beyond their normal parameters, the 358 cubic inch powerplant failed with catastrophic results. The engine builder found himself nursing burns and injuries on a night when most people are concerned with nothing more than champagne and kisses at midnight.

When SVT powertrain development engineer Dave Dempster hears the tale, he nods knowingly.

"The dyno never takes a holiday," he states, the voice of experience.

With a mind-boggling laundry list of changes in hand, Bill Lane's SVT powertrain team would find holiday time to be in short supply throughout late 2000 and 2001 if they had any hope of delivering a durable and imposingly powerful supercharged motor within the Terminator program time constraints.

The first powertrain program decision, though, was to conceptually leverage the work SVT had already dedicated to its highly-successful supercharged performance version of the F-150 pickup, the SVT Lightning.

"We went right off the Lightning, because the Lightning was robust, and there wasn't enough time to develop a new platform," acknowledges Cobra program manager Tom Bochenek.

"A lot of the stuff was based off of that," powertrain engineer Brian Roback says of the concepts passed from the Lightning to the Cobra. "That whole supercharger and intercooler system was revised for packaging constraints and such, but the basic concept was the same."

A cast iron block, forged pistons, Eaton roots supercharger, Manley connecting rods – the list of upgrades to the Terminator engine led to an obvious conclusion: not only was this engine both fearsomely powerful and reliable, it was also a relative bargain. Today's Terminator owners still thank SVT for going the extra mile in pulling together this component package. *Photo: Ford Motor Company*

But bringing concept to reality was to be a huge challenge.

"We looked at all the analytical data, put everything on the table that we had," affirms Cobra team manager Primo Goffi. "We had an opportunity to make one decision based on everything we knew at that point in time. We put our best foot forward, and we had one shot."

"We were meeting the horsepower target, the intent of the program," Dave Dempster says of the 340-hp naturally aspirated engine that would have been the heart and soul of the 2002 Cobra. Now with the supercharger looming, it was back to square one.

"From a development perspective it really put a crunch on us," admits Dempster, "because now we had to go through a whole litany of Design Verification tests to find out which hardware we could use, and what was going to survive and what wasn't."

John Coletti knew that breakage was to be an integral part of the process that would deliver him the supercharged engine he demanded for SVT's flagship vehicle.

"As you break the engines, it's almost like a chain – you pull on it, it breaks, you fix that link, you keep fixing all the weak spots," Coletti says. "And then finally, you've got a robust piece."

But first came the identification of the components that would make up the new Cobra powerplant. Though the Lightning would serve as functional inspiration, the situation was inarguably a complicated one.

"As far as what was changed and redesigned in terms of the engine, it's significant," Goffi notes. "From the oil pan and the scraper system, on the oil pan the front cover had to be redesigned. Cylinder heads, camshaft, upper

Although the supercharged SVT F-150 Lightning donated its basic architecture for the 2003 Cobra engine, a major redesign was needed to fit the massive motor into the Cobra body.
Photo: Frank Moriarity, Marcie Cipriani

and lower intake, intercooler, induction system, throttle body – it's a high percentage of parts on the engine alone that were all brand new."

Also new was a proposed ram air concept, that was actually taken to a prototype stage.

"We had laid back the radiator and such, and a did a nose entry ram air system, but the air and water management was difficult given the shape of the car," says Brian Roback. "The cost of doing the front structure unique like that started to become prohibitive as well, and about the time we were investigating that was when we went with the supercharger."

"When you're working within the existing architecture of a vehicle that's been around for a few years, you can't just suddenly tilt the radiator thirty degrees," Dempster agrees.

But feeding air to the supercharged engine was indeed a primary concern of the team as development got underway in earnest.

"We had the same general concerns that any boosted application has," Dempster points out. "There were engine sealing concerns, so we developed a new head gasket, which in turn drove a new head bolt for more clamping force. That was an expensive proposition, but it was required, it was necessary."

Compression of the air for combustion was crucial to the engine's ability to make power.

"We also did some fine tuning on the cylinder block itself," Roback explains. "The machining was adequate for low horsepower production kind of stuff, but when we started putting this kind of horsepower through it, we found the cylindricity of the bores was very critical.

"We started out basically with Lightning pistons, figuring they'd be pretty close," he continues. "We started out there, and we started stuffing a lot of pistons, basically because more heat was generated by the Cobra because of the higher rpm. So we had to change the machining of the piston itself to take care of that expansion rate, so that once it did expand, it did fit right and it didn't scuff. So it was a lot of development in that regard, too. It's not just like going to the aftermarket, slapping a blower on, and hoping for the best."

And it was here that the biggest problems to plague the Terminator engine would begin to rear their heads.

"One of the big differences between this program and the Lightning were the piston speeds," Dave Dempster notes. "Since this engine revs higher, that was a big concern. That was the weak link."

"A lot of the hardware hadn't been tested at that kind of level before," Roback says, "and no one knew the ultimate strength of these things except for what was on paper."

Running Wide Open

Much of the realization of SVT designs is accomplished in partnerships with Roush Industries, the multi-million dollar business formed by automotive legend and NASCAR team owner Jack Roush. In fact, a Roush building complex near the Detroit Lions' practice facility hosts SVT's headquarters. Roush specialists work with SVT to actually build engines, body parts, and chassis components, proving design validity long before production is ever scheduled.

For the Terminator, Roush was responsible for the attainment of the engine components and attaching parts such as the cooling system and exhaust. Roush also performed component engineering and subsystem

Inside the inner sanctum. The building is called Roush 57 and it's an unassuming structure in Dearborn, Michigan where SVT and Roush Industries devise some of the most exciting Ford vehicles.

work on electrical systems and the rotating assemblies. Roush and SVT further interfaced together on the intake manifold in conjunction with Eaton, the supplier of the supercharger.

In this process, SVT specifies to Roush the overall engine assumptions and performance parameters, and SVT also dictates testing. Calibration engineers from Roush also worked with Dave Dempster on fuel-related engine concerns.

Working with Roush, SVT's powertrain team put the pieces together that they believed would serve as the lifeblood of the Terminator. Indeed, the Design Verification builds – engines assembled with hand wrenches to ensure all parts fit and would hold together – went well.

SVT on occasion uses dynamometer equipment at the Roush facility in Livonia, Michigan, particularly when heavy demand on the internal Ford dynos might cause a program verification delay. Regardless, the dyno provides an accurate measure of an engine's performance. This is obtained by bolting the engine to a stand and attaching instrumentation. The engine is then run while subjected to a loading device which places resistance on its output.

"Once I get to twenty-five hours, I light my cigar," John Coletti says of the battery of multi-hour dyno tests that SVT engines are subjected to. "I know that the rest of it will be other issues, but it won't be a design issue. The first twenty-five hours tells you if you have a system that is robust enough to live."

The design of the Terminator engine was indeed sound. How powerful was the engine? Those who were there recount the first time the beast was mated to one of the dynos at Ford's Romeo, Michigan engine facility. The eight-hour burn-in period went fine, but when the dyno sensed it was time to open things up, the Terminator's furious power at wide open throttle simply overwhelmed the dyno. Accustomed to measuring sedate sedan and sport utility engines, the Terminator sent the hapless dyno into an emergency shutdown mode.

But that very power – so desirable for the Terminator program – soon presented a problem of vast proportions. Making boundless power with an engine was one thing, but making it last was another. And for the Terminator engine to reach production-ready status, it had to survive a vicious 300-hour dyno test, known in SVT circles as the FIE test. "FIE"

stands for Ford in Europe, referring to the origins of specialized testing that pushes engines to their limits – and beyond. SVT took the original tests and heavily modified them to meet their needs.

"Those tests were not designed for boosted applications – you know, a quick spurt up to this rpm, then stay there, and then back down," Dave Dempster explains. "So we basically came up with our own procedure that was more stringent than the original one. Because we need to prove out those additional components, like the supercharger and the intercooler."

"One of the test procedures that we had would have had the supercharger on full boost for hours – and that's an impossibility," points out Brian Roback. "For one thing, we found out we would drain the fuel in about two or three minutes, from a 20 gallon tank at full boost. So we had to go back and say, 'You know, this is not realistic. We're doing it at an accelerated rate, and we're doing that because it accelerates to there, but we also have to keep in mind that you can't physically do this out on the road. You can't stay in the boost for three minutes because you don't have the fuel and you don't have the road to do that...' You don't think three minutes is a very long time, but at full boost and 150 some mph? A lot of those tests, we go into them and we go through them and say, 'OK, what makes sense for SVT? This needs to be more stringent, while this needs to be more realistic as to how this vehicle functions...'"

But honing the FIE test for feasibility did not alter the biggest parameter – the 300-hour duration. As Tom Bochenek notes, "We had cars driving around, but we never broke anything in the cars – it's the dyno test that is so brutal. To me that was the turning point. To get the engine to pass, that was it."

And the engine was not passing. Indeed, far from it. The Terminator's massive power was too much for the connecting rods that had been more than ample for the 2001 Cobra and the proposed 2002 model. Of the twenty Terminator engines built in the Design Verification stage of the program, as many as ten were destroyed by devastating failure in attempts at the FIE test.

"The production previous-generation Cobra connecting rods, we broke them I don't know how many different ways," recalls Primo Goffi. "We had ones that came out the bottom of the engine, out the side of the engine... We found a weak link during our durability testing that caused a

2003 MUSTANG COBRA
4.6L 32v DOHC

UAW

Ford

Displacement : 4.601cc (280 cu.in)
Bore/Stroke : 90.2 mm X 90.0 mm
Compression Ratio : 8.5 : 1
Peak Power : 390 hp @ 6000 rpm
Eaton Supercharger @ 8.0 psi
Peak Torque : 390 ft-lb @ 3,500 rpm

Ford **SVT**
Experience

REP Visual Graphics

lot of grief and a lot of aggravation. You know how they always say there are a few defining moments in a program? Well, that was one of them – trying to pass our engine durability."

"A lot of it is getting set up, getting the right calibration," says Dave Dempster of the 300-hour test. "If the calibration's not right, you can just ruin a test. If you run it lean, or if you do something wrong… If you've got 150 hours in there and all of sudden something goes lean in the calibration and you waste a motor, you've just wasted all that time. So to get it up and running and broken in, there's a lot of support that has to take place."

"On FIE, basically it alters between peak torque and max horsepower," Brian Roback explains, "so it's going back and forth between those two points for the whole test, the whole 300 hours."

The tortuous conditions and stress placed on the engine are mind-boggling.

"You go by the dyno cell when that thing's running, and it's just screaming," Dempster says. "When you're in that cell, if you're physically inside that cell when the engine's running, it's just, 'Wow.'"

The scarred walls of dyno facilities offer mute testimony to the horrific damage that can be done when an engine fails under extreme testing conditions.

"When they go at high rpm, it is pretty destructive," Dempster says.

Adds Roback, "If an engine's running at 6500 rpm and something lets go…" The ominous conclusion is left to the imagination.

Cost Becomes No Object

With the angry force of the Terminator engine hurling connecting rods like shrapnel, the entire program was suddenly in doubt. Though Ford Engineering had a stronger connecting rod under development, SVT could not afford to wait for the program's conclusion and certification process.

"There were a hundred of what you'd tend to think of as more 'normal' problems in the program," Primo Goffi says, "but as far as the defining

ones, the engine was enormous. On any given day that was touch and go, to the point where we didn't know if we were going to have a program or not. We were getting to the point where it was 'something better happen' – we'd better figure out a way to get out of the box in some of the areas of engine durability because it was getting to the point where we were out of time."

"The production rods looked fairly marginal, and we thought, 'Well, let's give them a try – no one's really tested them to see,'" Brian Roback says. "And we saw. They were not sufficient. So we had to get something quickly and strong, and there was really nothing within the company that was available to fit that bill. We had to find something that existed to put in there, and that's when Manley came along."

Manley Performance Products Inc. makes connecting rods that stand up to the rigors of the most brutal high performance demand in motorsports: the top competition series of the National Hot Rod Association. Their connecting rods could survive in the world of the Terminator's supercharged powerplant – but it would be survival that came at a steep price.

"That was a huge cost decision," John Coletti emphasizes. "In the Ford Motor Company system, that would never have gotten the light of day. It was just so outrageous. To give you an example, our rods cost us maybe six dollars each. Those are $56 each. Do you know what fifty-six times eight is? That's our cost. But once we got down to this issue, the rods kept breaking and we said, 'We're going to get rid of that problem. Put the gold-plated part in there.' And that's a gold-plated part," he says, referring to the high cost of the solution.

That Coletti could make such a decision on his own speaks to the reputation of SVT and the confidence that the stakeholders have in the team. Referring to group vice president Bob Rewey, Coletti remembers,"He told me, 'Look, Coletti – just make it work.' OK, well, if that's the answer – I'll make it work."

To help further strengthen the engine, a decision was made to go with a nearly indestructible cast iron block, rather than the aluminum block found in the 2001 Cobra.

"It was only a little bit more durable, but you know, at that point, I had to go with that best parts I had," Coletti emphasizes. "At that point we'd just

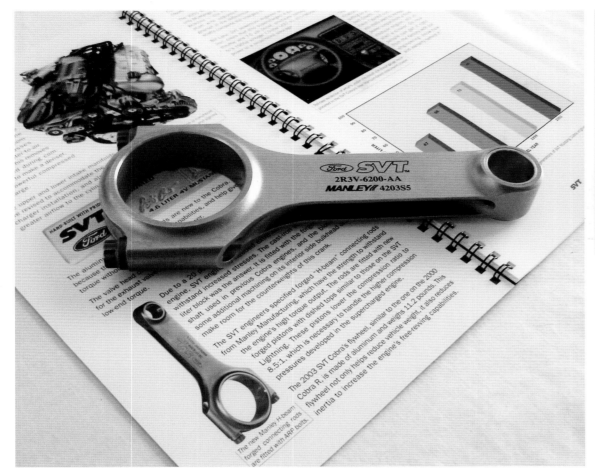

Left: Manley Performance Products have supplied one of the most critical engine components – connecting rods – to many of the most fearsome ground-pounders of the National Hot Rod Association. SVT knew that incorporating this competition heritage into the Terminator program would prove to be a wise decision.
Above: One of the actual Manley connecting rods that survived the grueling 2003 Mustang Cobra engine endurance tests became a prized souvenir in John Coletti's office. "It's not a very pretty trophy," Coletti admits, "but I remember exactly, saying I want one of those rods."
Photos: Frank Moriarty

spent all this money on the rods, so do you want to go with this block that's just five or ten percent less capable? I say no. It had nothing to do with money – hell, if it had anything to do with money I never would have put these rods in there. I'll tell you, two of these rods cost more than a whole block."

Reinforced with the Manley rods and the iron block, the powertrain team sweated out another 300-hour session for the Terminator engine. The results of this run are born out by the Manley rod found in John Coletti's office, a metallic memento of the test's successful conclusion.

For the Terminator, at last, all systems were go. Coletti would not have had it any other way.

"I can honestly say in hindsight there wouldn't have been many people in his shoes that would have kept on going with this program," Goffi says of SVT's leader. "We broke a lot of pieces, we had a lot of failures, and I know a lot of other people would have just thrown in the towel. John's got a pretty big whip, for lack of a better term. This car was going to happen. And he provided a lot of inspiration for the troops – along with that large whip that he carried! Everybody rallied together and pulled it off."

"We thrive under pressure, basically," Dave Dempster says. "Each package presents it's own unique challenges. And of course, working for John, you never know what he's going to pull out of the hat. I think that's what's great about this whole group."

Getting in Gear

With the Terminator engine's durability issues finally resolved, it was time to assess the results of SVT's powertrain agenda. New aluminum alloy cylinder heads provide better flow to feed the hungry engine, one that's officially – and extremely conservatively – rated at 390 horsepower at 6,000 rpm and 390 foot-pounds of torque at 3,500 rpm, compared with the 2001 model's 320 hp at 6,000 rpm and 317 foot-pounds of torque at 4,750 rpm. The Manley rods are mated with a forged-steel crankshaft, and the engine also boasts an aluminum flywheel similar to those found in the 2000 SVT Mustang Cobra R. At the engine's rear is a TTC TREMEC T-56 six-speed manual transmission. Behind that, an aluminum drive shaft with upgraded universal joints connects to the rear axle.

With those specifications locked in, all that remained was to address the details that would provide the vehicle its operational individuality, including the final gear ratio.

"The Lightning engine is running at lower speeds," John Coletti notes in comparison to the new Cobra. "She only whips up to 5200, 5300 rpm. It's a different system, because you've got the automatic transmission which is multiplying all the torque – it's a different set up.

"With the Cobra, when we first put this blower package together we had it scheduled to go to 6900 rpm," he continues. "We could have gone and got some real heavy duty horsepower – the problem was, first gear? We were driving around and you could stay in first gear up to 76 mph! It was too tall, I guess is the way to put it.

"So we said, 'That isn't going to work – it just doesn't feel right.' The engine is sitting there and it will carry you forever. Then we went from a 3.27 to a 3.55 (gear ratio), and that felt better. But we said, 'You know, it still doesn't feel right. We need to go ahead and bias the blower so it will pull a lot more torque early.' So it was just a matter of tuning. But we were trying to get it so it feels right, so it feels like a big engine, without having to take you to 6900 rpm. It was pulling huge horsepower."

But like the engineer that he is, Coletti is also justifiably proud of the efficiency of the Terminator.

"It's not only powerful, it's efficient," he states of the Cobra's twenty-two mpg highway rating. "And that's a message that people forget. It doesn't have the kind of glamour, but from an engineering standpoint, that's starting to show that you're good. The point here is that it's not only just power, because I always tell my guys you've still got to be socially responsible. If we were pissing away fuel and getting eight miles to the gallon, it catches up to you. People can point to you and say you're a low life and not socially responsible and everything else. The fact that we've got a combination now that does that is really kind of cool."

But before the Cobra could begin to display its highway efficiency, there was more testing to be done. Now, the vehicle dynamics team had the real Terminator engine available. It was time to head for the racetrack.

2003 *SVT*

Mustang COBRA

Configuration
Longitudinally mounted, 90-degree V-8,
cast iron block with aluminum heads,
fully counterweighted forged crankshaft

Bore x Stroke
90.2mm x 90.0mm

Displacement
4,601cc; 280 cu. in.

Compression ratio
8.5:1

Horsepower
390 @ 6,000 rpm

Torque
390 @ 3,500 rpm

Specific output
84.8 horsepower per liter

Redline
6,500 rpm
(fuel shut-off occurs at 6,500 rpm)

Valvetrain
Double overhead camshafts,
chain drive to exhaust cams,
secondary chains from exhaust to intake cams,
roller finger followers with hydraulic lash adjustment,
oval-wire beehive-shaped valve springs, four valves per cylinder

Intake valves
2 per cylinder, 37mm head diameter

Exhaust valves
2 per cylinder, 30mm head diameter

Fuel system
Sequential electronic fuel injection

Induction system
Eaton™ Corporation Generation IV Roots- type
supercharger with water-to-air intercooler

Boost pressure
8.0 psi maximum

Intake manifold
Cast aluminum, tuned equal-length runners

Throttle body
57mm twin bore

Mass-air sensor
90mm diameter

Exhaust system
Dual, stainless steel, 2.25-in. diameter; 3.0-in. polished exhaust tips

CHAPTER 6 TO THE LIMITS

Logging Track Time

Tom Chapman, Mark Dipko, and the other SVT chassis engineers had begun their tuning efforts using 2001 Cobras with improvised ballast designed to simulate the 655-pound weight of the Terminator engine. But that's all it was – a simulation.

"One of the issues was that we couldn't really get the weight in the right spot," says engineer Enzo Campagnolo. "We thought that we had something that was pretty close, but when we got the real motor it still wasn't exactly as we thought it was going to be."

Testing to date had taken place with a Workhorse Prototype, basically a proving foundation for rough components and designs under revision. Now the program evolved to the Attribute Prototype phase, with cars built by Roush using designs and components that were edging toward final specifications. Most importantly, under the hoods of the newer APs were real Terminator engines. It was time to get extremely busy.

"The first thing was the tires," says Cobra lead chassis engineer Mark Dipko. "Dean Martin, my partner/mentor on the 2000 Cobra-R, and I had always pushed to put 275 tires on the Cobra – and everyone told us it was impossible. I set that as my personal mission, because any less tire in the

Opposite: A 2003 10th Anniversary SVT Mustang Cobra undergoes track testing at Ford's Dearborn Proving Grounds. Above: The Terminator engineering team stands with an early prototype at Road Atlanta in 2001.

front would cause too much understeer on the front and a serious lack of traction on the rear.

"I enlisted my fellow SVT engineers and drivers in some of the grueling test track work of lap after lap around our handling courses in Dearborn and Naples, FL, as well as other tracks such as Grattan and Road Atlanta," Dipko says.

The team tested dozens of tire construction improvements submitted by candidates Goodyear and B.F. Goodrich.

"In the end, it was a very tough choice," Dipko admits, "because the tires had improved so much and we almost couldn't believe the performance difference. Although the Goodyear F1 looks the same on the outside, it is a completely new compound that stretched Goodyear's capabilities – and they delivered."

But during testing a new problem appeared, this time related to the newly-selected Goodyear tires' much larger size.

During Road Atlanta testing in early 2001, a supercharged Terminator engine fills the forward compartment of a highly-modified 2001 model year Mustang Cobra.

"At Road Atlanta, the front tires were hitting the tops of the wheel wells over the curbing and the rears were rubbing on the pinch flange," Dipko recalls. So severe was the front rub that the tires were abrading through the wheel well material and into the Terminator's wiring lines.

"This looked to be a disaster and the program manager wanted us to go back to the stock wheels fearing we could never get the 275s to fit. After some head-scratching, I determined that the bump stops used in the front shocks were out of spec and much too soft. This allowed the wheel to travel past its limit causing the contact with the wheel well. A frantic call to Bilstein led to a change to the bump stops… one problem fixed.

"Now for the rear," Dipko continues. "Our CAD analysis showed this potential interference and the data never lies. So I decided to take on something previously considered taboo – asking DAP (the Dearborn Assembly Plant, where the production Cobras would be constructed) to modify the sheetmetal. After a meeting with the engineers and

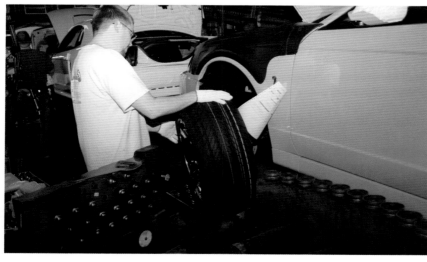

Issues with the Terminator's tire size were identified during testing and were solved on the assembly line, leading to changes made to the sheet metal for all Mustangs starting in 2003.
Photo: Marcie Cipriani

management at the assembly plant, they indicated there were several options to eliminate the interference and they would study the best approach. Within two weeks, they had a plan to make a small cut out at the back of the pinch flange on all Mustangs, to make room for the massive Terminator tires. If you look closely, you can spot this on any 2003 or newer SN95 model."

Testing in the SVT neighborhood took place at the Dearborn Proving Grounds Handling Course, a 1.1-mile, two-lane combination of short

straight-aways and a combination of 200-, 300-, 400-, and 500-foot constant radius turns.

"It's not a very sophisticated layout but it doesn't have to be for engineering work because we're most interested in the transience between steady state events – steady state straight, and the steady state corner," explains chassis systems supervisor Tom Chapman. "It gives us a good consistent test bed to do our evaluation work for tuning purposes."

"A lot of the handling development was done right at this track," Enzo Campagnolo says of the Dearborn facility. "And in this car, a lot of emphasis was put on max handling… Basically, we have a lap time objective that we are trying to meet. And a lot of it was done on this surface. All of the ride roads here are used. Pretty much this whole facility, plus tire supplier facilities, our test track in Romeo at the Michigan Proving Grounds, Road Atlanta was another track we used, Phoenix International Raceway – so we do use racetracks a lot to develop this type of vehicle."

Indeed, it is at the racetrack facilities that the Terminator passed its most grueling tests – two eight-hour durability tests.

The first such test took place late in February, 2001 at Road Atlanta. SVT traveled with two initial Attribute Prototypes based on the 2001 Cobra platform, red and black coupes. Under their hoods were early supercharged engines of the near-final Terminator design, but with the standard production connecting rods that caused the powertrain team such headaches.

The second eight-hour test was conducted at Firebird International Raceway in Phoenix almost exactly a year later, using a far more advanced 1PP prototype vehicle. Based on the finalized chassis specifications for engineering sign-off, this red coupe was complete with a Manley-rod-equipped engine.

Chassis engineer Jeff Grauer notes that during these eight-hour tests the cars are being consistently driven in the upper tenth of their maximum capability. The testing Cobra is set up with telemetry from car to crew, and the engineers can advise the driver about things like maintaining operation within desired rpm ranges.

"That's eight hours of actual on-track time," Grauer says. "We take out pit time, we take out everything except eight hours of actual at-speed testing.

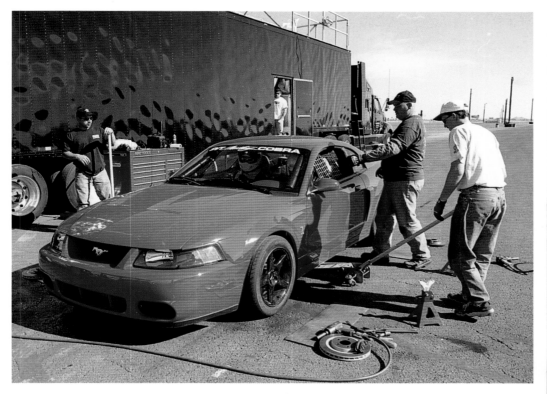

An eight-hour endurance test on a confirmation prototype at Firebird International Raceway, part of the battery of testing that proved the readiness of the Terminator.
Photo courtesy Enzo Campagnolo

When we did the second eight-hour it was 500 miles, right at 500 miles of track time. And that's a lot of track time."

"And we're not messing around," Tom Chapman adds. "We're balls out."

That can be proven by the quality of driving talent in SVT. Ford uses a four-tier global test driver rating system, with Tier Four having the most demanding qualifications. Of the thirty-four Tier Four drivers world-wide, six are found in the handful of Ford employees who make up SVT.

The eight-hour figure for these tests was chosen arbitrarily, but is more than enough to cover any potential on-track activity applied by a Cobra owner. After all, how many Cobra owners will have hour after hour after hour of racetrack time at their disposal, like SVT did during the day-and-a-half each such test consumed?

"And there's a lot of other testing," adds Campagnolo. "When we developed this car, there's a complete durability test that this car had to go through. That's run at our Michigan Proving Grounds, and that's a brutal test. And this car was no exception – it had to go through all of those requirements as well as fuel economy and cooling tests that are done all over the country."

"We have to meet the same engineering sign-off criteria as all mainstream Ford Motor Company products," Chapman points out. "We don't get exceptions because we're a small team doing something special."

"So we've got to meet all of the baseline stuff required by any vehicle, and then we test over and above to our own more extreme criteria as well," Campagnolo concludes.

Though the overall vehicle dynamics character of the Terminator was well established, the lengthy track stints and additional tests did reveal some areas that demanded improvement.

"We made some changes to the brake linings after this," Campagnolo reveals, "and we found we needed high temperature seals on the front and rear tie rod ends – because they basically melted right off the car! On the front now it has a greaseable joint."

Aside from these minor and easily corrected issues, the Terminator hungrily devoured lap after lap on the racetrack, just as Tom Chapman's team hoped it would.

"Other than wear items – tires, brake pads, things like that – we did not have any failures on either of our eight hour tests," Chapman states.

The Terminator's engineering sign-off came just six months before production, when all of the major components and designs were locked in. Still, minor tweaking went on beyond that date.

"Usually it starts out with the engineer who actually tuned it gets something that they like," says Jeff Grauer. "Then one or two of us will go on rides, drives, do some handling tests. We might throw some opinions out there, might make some minor tweaks. And then more of the team comes in – it just keeps getting bigger. But you don't have a lot of people giving opinions until you're pretty much done, and then it's a jury evaluation of, is it where it needs to be or does anything need to be tweaked?"

Tom Chapman felt that Mark Dipko's initial tuning of the new Cobra was too closely aligned with the competition focus of his previous project, the Cobra R.

"The big jury didn't get in the car and say, 'Whoa! You guys gotta back off,'" Chapman relates. "The rest of us told Mark, 'Dude, you've got to back off – this is, like, too much!' It handled great, but you're going to kill people – you'll knock them unconscious with this ride!"

Dipko, who felt that a competition feel is exactly what SVT's target market desires, begs to differ.

"I certainly disagree that the car was too harsh," Dipko states. "It was benchmarked against the BMW M3 and Camaro SS – and the subjective ride ratings were better than either of those vehicles… So it is all relative."

In the end, Dipko feels that he pointed the Terminator in the direction that SVT's most important jury – the Cobra buyer – demands from the performance group.

"I developed the car for the enthusiast, and they are willing to give up some ride comfort for overall handling performance feel."

Dropping the Hammer

While the Cobra was flogged on racetracks and handling courses in locations throughout the United States in pursuit of handling perfection, there were even more punishing tests facing the vehicle's mechanical systems.

One aspect exposed to such demanding scrutiny was the Terminator's clutch, provided by the Transmission Branch of well-known automotive supplier Valeo.

"Part of our standard verification testing that we do with new components – especially when we had a brand new clutch, and a new flywheel, and the 3.55 gear that we put into this – you have to run through a whole gamut of testing that the suppliers themselves will do, but then we also do stuff like stall tests, to see how many cycles that the clutch will take," explains SVT engineer Mike Luzader. "You basically park the car up against a fixed object – park it against the wall – and you let the clutch out at a particular rpm, like 2500 rpm, and basically stall the engine. There's a Ford test to see how many times you can cycle it before you actually fail the clutch on the vehicle. It's a way of testing the durability of clutch components."

Anyone who has smelled the pungent aroma of a burnt clutch can only imagine the stench of this cruel test, and Luzader confirms that, "you just can't ever get the smell out." Most test vehicles are destroyed at the end of their duties, and the clutch car was among the first Terminators to meet such an inglorious end.

"Tests like this can be done either at the suppliers' location, where we'll supply a vehicle to the supplier to do the testing," Luzader says, "or we can run the test up at Michigan Proving Grounds. Or we'll even have our own guys do it themselves. We do a drag cycle, where guys will do drag starts with it – do so many drag starts, and then they also have wide open throttle cycles that they have to run through."

For the Terminator, up to 1500 drag starts were launched, putting unbelievable strain on the powertrain. As Tom Chapman notes, "That's without parts changes. One of the guys gets in the car, goes out, and does non-stop, back-to-back, side-step the clutch, mother-lode drag starts."

To a muscle car fan, this may sound like a dream job. Jeff Grauer isn't so sure.

"They went through three sets of tires, and tank after tank of fuel to do 500 of these. I've done it in the Lightning, and it's fun – for about the first two minutes," Grauer laughs.

CHAPTER 7 DETAIL ORIENTED

**Opposite:
2003 Cobra in
Silver Metallic
Above: Mike
Luzader, Celeste
Kupczewski,
Scott Tate and
Nick Terzes
(left to right)
all played key
roles in the
development
of the
Terminator, with
responsibilities
ranging from
wind tunnel
testing to vehicle
seat design.**
*Photo: Frank
Moriarty*

The Components of a System

From its Manley-equipped supercharged engine to its robust TREMEC six-speed transmission, the Terminator's powertrain had stood up to everything thrown at it in a battery of arduous mechanical tests. And that power was now graced by a finely tuned suspension, one that overcame the front-heavy characteristics of the supercharger-and-iron-block combination. This Cobra lithely slithered around road courses at exhilarating speeds, gripping the track surface securely.

But if SVT's new creation was to see its heady features presented to the world, there was an inevitable fact yet to be faced: there were literally hundreds of smaller components to be addressed, all demanding the attention of SVT's engineers.

A common misconception among the public at large is that the auto manufacturers do just that: manufacture everything that goes into their product offerings. In reality, though, there are hundreds of suppliers who provide parts and components to supplement what automobile manufacturers actually fabricate themselves. The assembly line then puts the parts together to complete the intricate jigsaw puzzle that is a modern automobile.

In the case of a small-production-volume niche vehicle like the Terminator, the role played by specialized suppliers is of even greater importance. But before the components can be specified and ordered, SVT has to decide exactly what they need – and these needs must fit within the constraints of the blizzard of federal and self-imposed regulations and guidelines that govern any auto manufacturing process.

Among the new apparatus SVT required were body parts. Camilo Pardo had designed a distinctive exterior for the Terminator, and that design demanded special front fascia manufacturing to provide an aggressive look from an aesthetic perspective and enhanced airflow from a functional standpoint. Further, a new hood and composite rear deck joined vertical rocker panels as supplier requirements, along with body-color folding side mirrors.

Inside the car, a new electroluminescent instrument cluster was specified – complete with a supercharger boost gauge – in addition to a Terminator-unique gear shift knob, foot pedals, and a new steering wheel. Even the trunk light had to be redesigned.

But perhaps the detail-level piece de resistance was found at the base of the windshield: the windshield wipers boasted a wind-tunnel tested, aerodynamic wing shape to keep the stalks firmly planted at speed.

Meetings of the Minds

Between the Terminator's powertrain and chassis issues – not to mention the growing list of specialized components – the weekly SVT project review meetings that occurred throughout the Cobra's development were anything but dull.

"How many Wednesday SVT meetings updating the entire team – sales, marketing, the entire extended team – were just doom and gloom for a long time?" team manager Primo Goffi asks in reflection.

"Every day there was a new issue that we had to solve," recalls project manager Tom Bochenek.

Since their beginning in 1993, all SVT Cobras received their own
distinctive design cues – some functional, some purely aesthetic
– that set them apart from other Mustangs. The Terminator was
no exception. On the outside, the car received a new front fascia
with enlarged grille openings, a unique hood with flow-through
scoops, a composite rear deck, vertical rocker panels, body-color
folding side mirrors and a unique integrated spoiler with built-in
stop lamp. Appointments inside included metal trim foot pedals,
a custom-grip steering wheel, leather-wrapped shift knob with
brushed-aluminum insert bearing the six-speed shift pattern, and
specially-illuminated instrument cluster gauging.

Photos: Ford Motor Company, Marcie Cipriani

For a production model that moved down the Dearborn Assembly Plant line for less than two years, the Terminator boasted an impressive palette of seat options – all springing from the inspiration provided by the DeTomaso Mangusta from decades earlier. Seen here are Dark Charcoal seats with Medium Graphite inserts (top left), Medium Parchment inserts (top center), Red Leather inserts – available only on the 10th Anniversary models (top right). Dark Charcoal inserts (bottom left), and shimmering Mystichrome-matching leather (bottom right) were introduced for 2004. No matter the colors, all of the seats were equally adept at keeping drivers in place under hard cornering.

Photos: Ford Motor Company, Marcie Cipriani

"We had a very short finite amount of time, and we had issues with everything," agrees Goffi. "So you'd get smacked in the head, fall flat on your face… That's kind of how the program went. There were a lot of times when it was, 'Oh my God, what are we going to do?' The team banded together, we had support, we had strong leadership – 'Keep going, guys – come on! We gotta keep going!' There was nothing that was going to stop us. We had a lot of setbacks, but we just kept soldiering on."

In the trenches were SVT engineers like Scott Tate, relying on a crucial ability to multitask. Juggling the development of overlapping Terminator facets, Tate oversaw a domain of tasks that ranged from placing scores of informational and warning labels on the new Cobra – ensuring federal safety compliance – to planning a limited distribution of Terminators for the export market. This latter task engendered its own list of details, such as developing kilometers-per-hour inserts for the instrument cluster.

Yet another focus of Tate's labors was the specification of something every Terminator driver would immediately notice: the seat.

"We wanted to increase support for cornering," Tate explains, "because we didn't feel the current Cobra seat or Mustang seat had enough lateral support. And we wanted to try to increase comfort – but a lot of times those two things do not go hand in hand."

Like his cohorts on the vehicle dynamics team addressing the car's "feel," Tate's biggest challenge came in facing the fact that seat comfort and support is completely subjective to each user; trying to equate intangibles into manufacturing specifics was a daunting assignment.

Once Tate had developed a prototype Terminator driver seat, he held evaluation tests comparing his seat against the 2001 Cobra seat and a Recaro competition-based seat – although as he notes, "If you get ten people in a drive evaluation, you'll get ten different opinions on what they think a 'good seat' is.

"It was a weekend drive," Tate continues, "and we had a prescribed route. We had rating forms that you filled out, and when all was said and done we saw which one rated best and started tweaking that design from there."

The seat testing hosted bodies ranging from the slight frame of Celeste Kupczewski to the imposing stature of John Coletti himself. Ironically, though, in the end the Terminator driver's seat was one finding its way home.

Tate looked to the late 1960s DeTomaso Mangusta supercar for his seating inspiration. While it's common knowledge that the Mangusta was powered by a Shelby-tuned Ford 289 V-8 engine, there was another Ford connection: designer Giorgetto Giugiaro and Alejandro DeTomaso had borrowed the seat design of the 1960s Mustang for the Mangusta.

"They basically 'insporterized' a stock Mustang seat," Tate laughs, "by putting more aggressive bolstering on it and things like that, and fit it into the Mangusta platform. And we saw the seat, and said, 'Hey look – it uses the existing structure, it's got basically what we're looking for – we can tweak that and get a good bang for the buck out of it.' And that's what we ended up using."

Building Enthusiasm

SVT's "bang for the buck" philosophy carried over into the team's selection of component suppliers – in the case of the Terminator seat, Visteon Corporation. But attracting suppliers to a project like the new Cobra was not necessarily easy, and sometimes required a combination of delicate persuasion and old-fashioned hard bargaining.

"If we want to do a certain component, sometimes it's difficult at the onset of a program because everybody's thinking big volume," Primo Goffi explains. "You have a lot of 'Big Three' suppliers, and if you're not doing 100,000 units minimum, they don't even want to talk to you."

"We're coming in there and we're saying, 'OK, we need you to do 10,000 units a year, and we need you to do it quicker than you would do it normally,'" SVT engineer Mike Luzader illustrates. "'And oh, by the way, because we're small and nimble, we want you to do it cheaper.' A lot of times suppliers don't want the business because it's just not financially to their benefit. Then we kind of strong-arm them into it, anyway."

"More and more these days suppliers can't cater to us, off in the corner playing with a few vehicles," Goffi admits. "It's a challenge. You run into that all the time with SVT programs – nobody wants to play ball with a few thousand units. It makes it tough, and it's expensive."

There were instances when a supplier willing to work with SVT on the new Cobra required indoctrination to the realities of the carved-in-stone Terminator target date.

"We have people that are not normally used to doing this kind of process – a shortened, tighter timeframe," says powertrain engineer Dave Dempster. "Especially when we get involved with purchasing people and supply type people, a big part of it is selling them on our way of doing business… We're not building three quarters of a million vehicles here – we're going to build 5000. We can't use the supplier that makes the F-series pickup part because they don't want to talk to us. So what we try and do is find the niche type suppliers, and then convince the people that make those decisions to allow us use them."

When a part available from a niche supplier is viewed as critical by SVT, sparks can fly.

"Sometimes we'll fight for low-volume suppliers that our own purchasing doesn't necessarily agree with, like Bilstein," chassis engineer Enzo Campagnolo says of the Terminator's shock supplier. "To get monotubes on this car was a little bit of a struggle. Our own purchasing didn't want to go along with it due to the costs, but from an engineering standpoint, we said we have to have these. And we didn't give up the fight, and we got them in the long run. We'll fight for the small volume supplier on parts like that, where there's an engineering reason."

The suppliers for the Terminator program were enlisted one by one, without being aware of exactly what it was that they were now part of – aside from the fact that it was a top-secret SVT program. Once the suppliers were on board, though, the overall scope of the Terminator project was revealed to them en masse in a clandestine presentation at a local hotel, where both the speed of the program and the power of the car to be built shocked many of the suppliers.

"We had a supplier kickoff meeting," Tom Bochenek recalls, "and there were all of the suppliers there. We went through the whole list of program assumptions, and even in that meeting, we had people saying, 'You want to do what?!?'"

"We brought them in, signed the confidentiality agreements," remembers Celeste Kupczewski. "Then John Coletti came in and Tom Scarpello came in. So we probably had 100, 150 suppliers in the room, and then we did the big presentation: 'Guess what, guys? You're working on a 400-horsepower Cobra.'"

While the marketing presentation – revealing the motivations behind the vehicle creation – was important, equally crucial was a presentation by Camilo Pardo. The designer explained how he had approached the theme of the Terminator, illustrating his comments with drawings and photos of the "clay car."

"We went through the whole list of program assumptions, and even in that meeting, we had people saying, 'You want to do what?!?'"
~Tom Bochenek

"We were really trying to get people just excited about it and passionate," says Kupczewski. "We made the suppliers want to be a part of the program. There's the 'cool factor,' that this is a good thing for them as well to be associated with such a high-profile vehicle as this."

Did the presentation work?

"A lot of these guys are gear heads, so they just jumped in with both feet," affirms Mike Luzader. "They just loved it!"

The depth of that enthusiasm is borne out by an enlarged print that Tom Bochenek proudly retained: a photo of the clay design car, signed by all of the suppliers present at the kick-off meeting.

The Crucial Partner

The vast majority of the suppliers who contributed to the DNA of the Terminator had worked with SVT or Ford in the realization of past projects. But it was a company that specialized in the automotive aftermarket – one new to the realm of OE (Original Equipment) suppliers – whose name would become nearly synonymous with that of the Terminator: Manley Performance Products.

Though Ford came to rely on Manley's connecting rods for the salvation of the Terminator's supercharged engine, it was Roush Industries that first recommended the supplier to SVT. Roush was already familiar with Manley's tremendous competition success designing critical engine components.

"They ran into a problem that they identified with the powdered metal connecting rod and its durability," Manley general manager Michael Tokarchik says of his first hearing about the Terminator. "So they called me in August 2001 and said, 'We've done some things together before, and we know that you're in a very strong position in the aftermarket, and we know that you potentially have a solution to our problem. Would you like to come out and meet with us?' So we had a couple of conversations in August, and things got pretty serious."

Initial discussions led to Manley supplying test rods to SVT and Roush for evaluation.

"We began discussions of the possibility of integrating our aftermarket connecting rod into their program," Tokarchik says. "Within a short period of time they took receipt of enough sets of connecting rods to, in essence, start again on the design validation. Because in the passenger car arena there is a very specific protocol as to what you must do in order to validate your engine and all the components within. So they began that almost immediately, saying, 'OK, let's at least get some engines built and then we'll have you out here and we'll start talking about the commercial side of things.'"

But before the discussions of finances and rod production could get underway, Tokarchik had to modify an existing Manley connecting rod for its new duties.

"The part that I was supplying to the aftermarket required three modifications," notes Tokarchik. "I had to change the crank bore size slightly, and we're talking tenths of a thousandths of an inch. I had to change the pin bore slightly, and I also had to change the pin bushing material. As you know, the Terminator engine is supercharged, and that boost was creating an extremely high cylinder pressure for a spark-ignited gasoline engine. The cylinder pressure was extremely high. And as a result, one of things that they had recognized even prior to having some of the connecting rods fail was a high rate of pin bushing wear. So I took an alloy that I typically use in NASCAR and I started making the pin bushings for the prototype rods.

"I was changing the pin bushing material in order to reduce the amount of pin bore wear due to two things, really," he continues. "Number one was the high cylinder pressures and number two was the limited amount of oil that gets up into that area of the piston and rod assembly when you're not using piston oilers. So that's how we launched the design validation and the testing scheme."

It wasn't like Tokarchik and the Manley team had the luxury of extended development time. This first foray into OE sales for a company that had always been an aftermarket supplier was taking place under the tightest of time constraints.

"This is a significant time compression when you're speaking about OE programs," Tokarchik agrees, "which typically have maybe twenty-four or thirty months to plan. Here it is October, and they want to start building engines in March."

As such, Tokarchik had to leverage what he already knew, much like the SVT engineers used the concepts of the Lightning engine as a launch pad for the Terminator powerplant.

"I had an existing OEM type program for a marine customer, and I had this running as what I would call a very good manufacturing model," Tokarchik reveals. "I knew what its output was, I knew how to scale up its output, I knew all the bottlenecks within the system. So basically what I did was I put together – in just a few weeks – a plan of taking this and scaling it up significantly in order to address the volumes of the Cobra program."

For Manley Performance Products, the Cobra program was an opportunity to enter a new, sizeable market. Larger engine component companies might look at the situation differently.

"There were a lot of people who were concerned for obvious reasons whether an aftermarket company like Manley could do this," Tokarchik readily concedes. "Obviously the Federal-Moguls of the world, the huge multi-billion dollar, multi-national corporations – these are the people who didn't want to do niche business because they didn't want to sign up any business unless it's two million rods per year. They don't want to deal with a volume smaller than that.

"Basically what I had to do was to take a look at the cell that I wanted to create, and the lead times for some of this equipment, and actually I had to go out and buy it before I had the purchase order from Ford. And I also had to do it on my own nickel, which made things pretty interesting."

Though some larger suppliers do shy away from niche programs like SVT's Terminator, others actively participate. Karl Schmidt Unisia (KUS) supplies the automotive world with a staggering thirty-million pistons per year world-wide, but they agreed to participate in SVT's small-volume niche program and supply the Cobra's power cell assembly: pistons, connecting rings, wrist pins and rings. This meant that Manley would actually be supplying KUS with the connecting rods, which would then be incorporated into the assemblies delivered to Ford's Romeo Engine Plant.

So Ford and KUS were placing their faith in an aftermarket supplier, while Manley was trusting that Ford would actually give the company its OE business – this was a potentially risky situation.

That the Romeo Engine Plant north of Detroit would one day be this well-stocked with Manley connecting rods was far from a given during SVT's Terminator planning. Both Ford Motor Company and Manley Performance Products found that faith and trust was a two-way street when it came to bringing what was traditionally an aftermarket supplier into the manufacturing flow of supercharged Mustang Cobras.
Photo: Frank Moriarty

"There was a tremendous leap of faith by all parties – and then we began," Tokarchik says. "During the month of December we started to configure the cell, we bought all of the fixtures and gauging and everything that we needed…

"We knew what we wanted, the commercial issues were behind us, the paperwork was going through the system to receive a purchase order," he continues. "So when we returned from Christmas holiday in January 2002, the first week we began production and we ramped up production through the month of January and into the month of February. So with the first shipments that we were making by the end of February, we were now filling the pipeline for Ford."

Both Ford and KUS typically deal with ISO-certified suppliers, and Tokarchik had to scramble to provide similar assurance to his new partners.

"Not only did we have to ramp up our production, build a sister cell, take care of all the commercial issues – but then we had to integrate a quality system into this which would mirror the formal quality system of an ISO-based organization," he concludes.

But all the effort proved to be worth it.

"It really was a tremendous leap of faith, but probably one of the best things that has happened to the company, to Manley Performance," Tokarchik assesses. "From there we were able to parlay our experience into some other opportunities – we have a connecting rod in the Ford GT, and there were some other things that we were able to do as well. And it was very good for us culturally as well, because it was the first time that we were really exposed to the passenger car activity culture. We've always been involved with the Big Three, but always on the aftermarket side or the racing side."

Cleared to Load

With suppliers verily signed up to provide substance to the Terminator, SVT's engineers turned their attention to detail upon detail, things that couldn't be allowed to fall through the cracks if the new Cobra was to make it to production.

One such item had to do with the new front fascia of the Cobra. Though being low and parallel to the ground gave the Terminator's snout a menacing aura, the validity of Camilo Pardo's design hinged on the answer to one unavoidable question – would it clear the loading process on a delivery truck?

To find out, SVT engineers found themselves in an empty lot, equipped with a car carrier and a 2001 Cobra bearing approximations of the Terminator front fascia. The car was loaded and unloaded, loaded and unloaded, the team searching for an answer to the question, "How low can you go?"

Another such detail arose late in the program. The Terminator was facing an expensive federal government Tier Two gas guzzler penalty – until a last second revision found the new Cobra migrating to the less-costly Tier One.

"This was going to be a Tier Two gas guzzler, which I think would have tacked a couple thousand dollars onto the price tag," Enzo Campagnolo relates. "We were trying to figure out how to get around that toward the end of the program. So, the car now has a shift light indicator on the dash – that makes it a Tier One gas guzzler. That's the only reason that light's there."

The warning indicator – which rather conservatively signals the driver when to shift up to the next gear – would eventually prove to be unnecessary. In the second year of production, the Terminator's federal fuel efficiency rating was re-certified, and the vehicle's Tier penalties were lifted. The Cobra wasn't really a gas guzzler after all – and that belated recognition was a retroactive victory for John Coletti's mandate of performance through efficiency.

CHAPTER 8 POWER PLANT

need for those items, basically on a moment's notice," says Mike Eller, who originally came to the Niche Line as Launch Manager.

Eller points to a late 1995 build as an example of the Niche Line's capabilities, when his team was asked to perform trial builds of four-valve engines for a potential Thunderbird project.

"I got an e-mail about the engines on a Wednesday, the parts showed up on Friday, and the following Monday we built six engines," Eller says. "We built those six engines absolutely problem-free with basically three days notice. On the High Volume Line that would have taken three to six months to be able to do something like that, and we did it in three days."

In 1999, the Niche Line was moved to its current remote building. Upon arrival in its new home, the line functioned by performing engine

Opposite: Terminator engines, ready for installation. Above: Selling signed t-shirts and other apparel was edging into rock star territory for Niche Line engine builders. But it was all for a good cause, as the profits generated by the sale of Romeo Engine memorabilia benefitted local charities.

Niche Market

Gary Hunt. RJ Kreiner. Bob McIntyre. Ron Anderson.

To dedicated followers and fans of SVT machinery, these names are nearly as recognizable as those of show business celebrities, for they and a handful of others make up the roster of the Ford Romeo Engine Plant's Niche Line.

Located north of Detroit, Romeo Engine is a huge, bustling plant where Ford standard production engines are built in massive quantities on the facility's High Volume Line. But in a smaller building to the rear of the plant, the pace is different. Here the powerplants of SVT's flagship vehicles are built by hand and then "signed" by the two-person team responsible for each engine's start-to-finish assembly.

The Niche Line was developed with the idea of manufacturing flexibility in mind, and was originally located in a segregated area within the main plant when founded in 1995.

"Literally where the name 'niche' came about was the fact that we were looking for niche type products that we would be able to go in and fill the

Mike Eller, who envisioned Romeo Engine Plant Niche Line operation, performs a quality inspection.
Photo: Frank Moriarty

ROMEO ENGINE NICHE LINE

HAND BUILT   QUALITY

4.6 L MUSTANG COBRA ENGINE

TEAM · PRIDE · QUALITY · CUSTOMER SATISFACTION

build-ups from a complete lower end block. In the five-letter code used to designate completion aspects of Ford's engine building, this was the work of C, D, and E assembly lines. The A-B builds took place on the High Volume Line in the main Romeo Engine facility.

"A-line installs everything involved in installing the crankshaft – main bearings, crank, various dowels for other components, and oil gallery cup plugs," explains Cary Kramp, Niche Line Coordinator. "When the engine leaves A-line, it is basically a block and crank ready for piston and rod install. B-line completes the short block. Pistons and rods are installed, the oil pump, windage tray, oil pump pickup tube, and oil pan. When the engines leave B-line, they are ready for head dowel/gasket install, and then the heads."

Having each engine's A-B process completed on the High Volume Line before passing it off to the Niche Line for completion worked fine for SVT's Cobra program – until 2001, when the Terminator suddenly began to loom large on the Niche Line's horizon.

Primo Goffi, SVT's Cobra team manager, knew from past experience that early communication with all of the team's support areas would be critical to make the Terminator a reality.

"There's a lot of back and forth – the amount of meetings that you have to have to ensure proper communications between us and the rest of the company is staggering," he notes.

But this exchange of information is especially important with entities like the Niche Line, where established procedures are already in place.

"You try to work with them concurrent to the design process, and design not only for performance but for assembly and manufacturing as well," Goffi stresses. "That's critical, because you can make the best design in the world, but if you can't produce it in volume it's not going to work. And you're careful because you don't want to disrupt the Niche Line because it effects the program financials as well. You've got to pay for new tooling, there's new machines, new processes at the engine facility – so it's really important that those guys are involved up front."

Phil Brooks and Al Gossett (right) and Ron Anderson and Bob McIntyre (far right) were two of the two-man assembly teams who were responsible for overseeing these engine blocks from initial preparatory steps to final completion.
Photos: Frank Moriarty

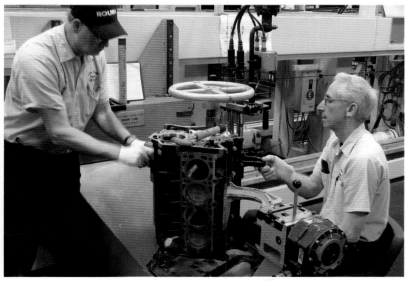

Making Room

While avoiding any disruption to an assembly line is the ideal, studies of the feasibility of the proposed Terminator engine manufacturing process pointed to some disturbing conclusions. Prior Cobra engines had essentially been built on standard blocks, but the supercharged Cobra was unique – and trying to complete the Terminator engine's A-B process on the High Volume Line looked as though it would lead to manufacturing chaos.

"The new crankshaft coming in for the Terminator engine – which is a steel crankshaft from Kellogg – would have thrown all kinds of complexity at their system in the High Volume Line and slow them down, which can't be done because they're the money maker for the plant," Cary Kramp acknowledges. "And the piston and rod assembly – our connecting rod bolts are 40/1000ths wider, center to center, than the standard two-valve connecting rod. And that throws in all kinds of tooling complexity and skill, trade, and maintenance types of complexity at their line, which they really can't afford."

"Even before then, this was something that was a thorn in the side of the High Volume Line," adds Eller, referring to the Cobra builds. "Because, if you think of it, it was a situation where if we were to build sixty Cobra engines using the A-B process on the High Volume Line, they would have to start and build sixty short blocks and take them out of the system at the end of the B line operation. And that would leave a huge hole of sixty engines in the rest of the line. Now, they would spread that out, running a batch of fifteen at a time, but still, it was a repetitive hiccup that would go through that assembly line every day."

The solution to the challenges presented by the Terminator was unavoidable: move the A-B process over to the Niche Line as well. For the first time, Cobra engines would be hand-built by the Niche Line teams from start to finish.

Left: This entire half of the current Niche Line had to be built in order for start-to-finish, by-hand Terminator engine assembly to become a reality. Below: The walls of the Romeo Engine Assembly Plant show the employees' pride of involvement in Ford's high performance history.
Photos: Frank Moriarty

"I went out there and asked them right at the very beginning of the program, asked the guys on the line: 'We're going to put on a supercharger. What do you think about it? If you guys have to put a supercharger on this thing, what about the weight?'" recalls SVT powertrain engineer Brian Roback. "You might think a lot of union guys would say, 'We don't want to do this or do that.' But you go out to that line, and they say, 'Supercharger? What's it going to weigh?' And you say, 'An extra 30 or 40 pounds.' And they say, 'Well, I don't care – is it going to make more

Tom Wilson, Brad Lammers and Cary Kramp (left to right) all labored under an intense deadline to meet the demands of bringing the 2003 Mustang Cobra to market.
Photo: Frank Moriarty

power?' 'Yes.' 'Put it on! We'll do it.' Any time I go out there and say, 'We want to change this, or we need to change that,' they just ask, 'Is it going to make it better? Do it!' They are all for it; they're really gung ho about it."

But moving the A-B processes from the High Volume Line and introducing these new components demanded more than mere enthusiasm. The Niche Line building required physical expansion to accommodate the new tasks, and new assembly stations – with powertrain hardware and software assembly systems developed by Johann A. Krause, Inc. – were also necessary. In the end, new Stations 15 through 21 would make up the A-B process on the north side of the Niche Line.

"We moved the whole building out and expanded the complex to make room for extra material handling – the blocks, the cranks, the racks and things like that," says Brad Lammers, the manufacturing engineer lead for Terminator. "But also, in the main assembly line, where the short blocks were built up before, they already had all the testing equipment that was integrated into the line. Integrating that test equipment and some of the alignment equipment that we use, like for the crank, into a manual process was challenging as well. For example, the piston stuffing: there are little details like metering the amount of oil in that step so we didn't throw off the test equipment. We had to make sure we were going to be building quality engines."

Indeed, it is the testing that is absolutely essential to successful engine building.

"There's a lot of in-process testing that goes on in the main line during the build-up of the short block, and for that matter the long block, just to make sure everything is correct," points out Tom Wilson, the manufacturing engineer lead for all Romeo Engine projects. "Any time you get to a certain stage of the engine after the crank and main bearings are all assembled, you do a torque-to-turn test to make sure everything is nice and smooth, and after the piston rods are assembled you also do a torque-to-turn test. After you run down the main bearing caps you do an end plate test on the crank to make sure that there's just enough movement in the crank but not too much. You test all these different seals to make sure that the oil is being contained after you button up the whole long block – you test the whole oil cavity, by pressurizing the cavity to make sure no oil can seep out. And you test the water cavity to make sure no water can get out."

"Well, none of that stuff was over here," Wilson says of the Niche Line. "Before, they were basically taking a product that was produced on the other line, bringing it over here, and dressing it by putting on the outside parts. We had to figure out a way to run all those tests within cycle time, along with all of the assembly."

Cycle time is the heart of an assembly line. It's the measure of how long the work-in-progress remains at a certain assembly point or station on the assembly line. To minimize cycle time while maximizing efficiency required meetings between SVT, Roush, and Krause engineers, as well as the actual engine builders of the Niche Line.

"That process was done in two kinds of meetings," explains Wilson. "We had an engine design review at Roush/SVT, where we'd bring members from the assembly team to review the product on a weekly basis and give our comments and direct them in their design. Say, 'No, this won't work – you have to change this a little bit so it's designed for manufacturing.' And then there was another type of meeting out at the supplier that produced the machinery that we use to assemble the engine, where we did the same sort of thing. We'd bring some of the team out there and sit down with their guys. We'd go back and forth on the concepts of the tooling and how it was going to be assembled."

"What was also really helpful was the 3-D modeling software that we've all moved into within Ford," adds Lammers. "You could show them a 2-D print and it was kind of hard to visualize. But when we'd show them an actual 3-D process, they could pull the part away, and then put it back in, to get the feel for how it would go together manually."

The Romeo Engine team began tightening the flow and usage of new equipment for the Terminator build process with a series of scout builds.

"We don't just toss it over the wall, by any means," states SVT engineer Brian Roback of the handoff of his team's design to the Niche Line's assembly crew. "We're there often. I think when we were doing the early engine builds I was literally out at Romeo for three weeks straight, pretty much every day – not even coming in to SVT's offices, just spending the time out there going through the assembly processes. I enjoyed it as much as they did, to tell you the truth."

"We would take an engine, put it on the line, and send it around before a lot of the tooling was in place," Tom Wilson says of these initial builds. "We'd assemble it by hand using the repair bay techniques and we'd look at prints of how we were going to use the tools in production. During the scout builds we'd try to visualize how that was going to work and whether our concept was on the right track. And we'd send the scout engine around at different stages when different levels of tooling were available, and it helped a lot."

"Obviously, one of the major changes was the intake manifold install," Cary Kramp points out. "Before, it used to go on in two pieces as a naturally aspirated intake manifold. We had to integrate a hoist here to pick up an almost ninety-pound supercharger and lower manifold and intercooler assembly. It may seem minor, but it was pretty major. We had to put in a new track system to carry the weight of that tool.

"Then the other big challenge was our test equipment, for the oil cavity and water cavity air tests," he continues. "While we did do water cavity before, we did not do oil cavity before. That was pretty tough to set up – it's pretty tough to dial in, and it's really tough to find leaks, especially when they're internal to the oil cavity. And cold tests – the cold test was really tough to dial in."

The cold test turns the near-complete engine to check for accurate compression, cleverly making use of the fact that there is no need for combustion to measure compression.

"Our cold test assimilates compression by the amount of torque it requires to rotate the crank through the compression cycle," Mike Eller explains. "In simple terms, if there were a defect that would affect compression it would take less torque to turn the crank through the compression cycle. Of course, it's more complicated than that because we also look at rate of climb and rate of drop. We get a torque signature from each cylinder that looks like a tall, narrow bell curve. The signature is compared to an average curve, based on thousands of engine cycles, and accepted or rejected based on statistical limits. Much, much more reliable than manual compression readings..."

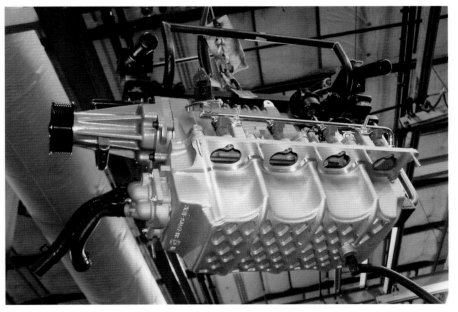

Hand-building Terminator engines was all about efficiency and easing repetition. Having builders manhandle heavy components like the Eaton supercharger seen here would never do. Instead, a custom hoist was designed that allowed the build teams to focus on correct installation.
Photo: Frank Moriarty

In addition to addressing mechanical issues, the Niche Line Coordinator and senior operators from the line were responsible for studying much of the actual process work, using Ford's Small Group Activities team concept.

"Balancing the line was one of the main things that the SGA team helped us with," Tom Wilson quickly acknowledges. "Simply saying, 'You know, it may not look like it to you guys, but this station has a lot of work in it and we can't do it within the cycle time. You need to move some of it off. And this station, it's got a whole bunch of parts listed on the bill of material that have to be put on here, but it really isn't that much because all these assembly processes go quickly.'"

"Even though the structure is in place, you're now getting down to the order of operations like the sequencing of bolts, which bolts are you putting on first, which parts are you putting on first," Brad Lammers says. "We knew all this stuff had to be completed at this station in order to move on, but some of it got rearranged."

"You've got to do it as a team," Wilson sums up. "These are the guys who have to live with the process and work with the process, day in and day out, after we're technically done with the project. So if you don't get their opinion and their buy-in into how you're developing the process, it won't

work. As engineers, it doesn't really matter to us if we do it as A or B – what matters is that it works and the operators agree with it."

The pride of the Niche Line engine builders is probably the most important asset of the operation. It was Mike Eller who came up with the concepts that effectively leverage that pride into quality engines.

"We had twenty guys, we had ten stations, and they were looking at having two guys per station," Eller recalls of the Niche Line's inception in 1995. "I said, 'Wait a minute, why don't we change that? Instead of having two guys

Paint by the numbers? Although the numerous assembly reference charts that decorated the Niche Line made Terminator engine-building seem like a purely logical process, the diagrams don't reflect the incredible attention to detail that each engine builder brought to the line.
Photos: Frank Moriarty

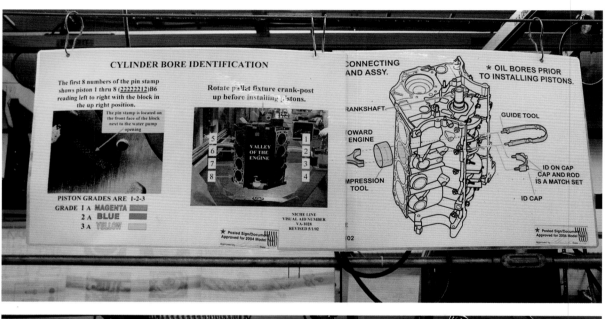

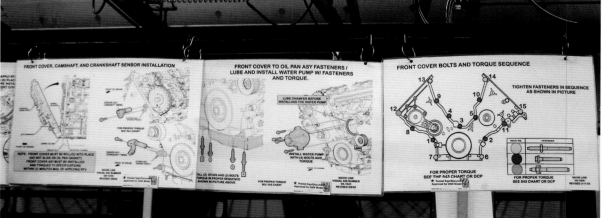

per station, from a pride and workmanship standpoint, why don't we have two guys per engine, and have each team build their own engine completely and follow the engine down the line?' And the launch team loved it.

"The other thing that I threw out there at the time was, to really, really optimize this pride and workmanship, was to allow these guys to actually sign the engine. To tell them, if you build this engine, it's your engine."

The concept evolved to the stamped metal plates – complete with the signatures of each two-man team – that eventually graced each supercharged Terminator engine. Indeed, the right to "sign" their work has become such a matter of pride that it is part of the United Auto Workers labor agreement covering the Niche Line activities.

Between the signatures and the fact that the new Terminator engines were to be complete builds from Ford's processes A through E, the Romeo Niche line was set to ascend to even greater prominence with the new Cobra.

"These guys put their names on it, and they want to be responsible and have the pride to do every bolt and every fastener and every dowel, and now they can," Tom Wilson says.

Late in 2001, the Niche Line's Terminator efforts finally reached the Process Verification stage, with roughly twenty engines built during this stage.

"We have to assemble the engine just like it's going to be assembled in production," Wilson says. "That's done normally six months before the first actual production engine is run on the line. We're ready six months before Job One. You have to be – you can't prove out the process unless you're assembling the engine like you're going to do at engine Job One."

Indeed, it was the Process Verification engines assembled on the Romeo Engine Niche Line that finally passed the tortuous 300-hour FIE dyno tests. With that success, the entire Terminator project moved into final "go" status.

It had been far from an easy task, but the Niche Line was production-ready for the Cobra. How did the Romeo Engine team feel about the Terminator project's compressed development timeline?

"If we've got a specific thing that we're working on and we have to launch a vehicle?" asks Cary Kramp. "Bam! We figure out what we've got to have, what we have to go after, and we go get it. We don't worry about deadlines – we beat the deadlines."

Engine builder Bill Sheffer rings a bell at the end of the assembly line to signal the completion of another Terminator engine.

Tony Frandle, Ken Bienkowski, Doug Campbell, Phil Brooks, Gary Smith, Al Gossett, Ron Anderson, Bill Sheffer, Paul Wormsbacher, Steve Foe, Jim Donovan, Bob Maskell, Dave Snider, Dale Berry, Jay Conklin, Keevin Ousley, Frank Cilluffo, Tim Parrott, Ann Lemay, Jeff Hamblin, Mark Schuman, Bob McIntyre, Gary Marston, Brad Hubbard, Cary Kramp. Not shown Bob Skovran Jr. and RJ Kreiner.

The unheralded heroes of the Romeo Engine Niche Line assembled for a end-of-production portrait with the last SVT Mustang Cobra engine. If you drive a Terminator, odds are a pair of these guys makes it go.

CHAPTER 9 UNDER COVER

Corralling the Workhorses

**Opposite:
Photographer
Nick Twork knew
he was seeing
something out
of the ordinary
when he grabbed
this shot of a
Terminator
prototype on the
prowl on July 2,
2001.
Above: Images
of two prototypes
drying off after
a morning rain
mysteriously
appeared on the
Blue Oval News
Web site in 2001.**

With early test engines coming off the Niche Line at Romeo Engine Plant, SVT needed Terminators to put them into. But the complex task of building iteration after iteration of prototype level vehicles had begun long before.

The prototype vehicles basically inhabit one of two domains: early test beds that are used for experimentation, proof of concepts, and component testing, followed by a series of later builds closely aligned with or even matching final production specifications.

"It's hard to put a handle on the Attribute Prototypes and the Workhorses, but over the life of the program we probably had over twenty vehicles," says Mike Luzader, the SVT engineer in charge of the prototype parade. "I wouldn't say we had twenty at one time, because we recycled cars in and out, in and out," he says. "You always want to try to keep the freshest stuff out there. And a lot of times when you run a test like the clutch/stall test, it pretty much destroys the vehicle because you get so much smell in the vehicle."

Although everyone from the vehicle dynamics team to the powertrain engineers are anxious to get their hands on prototype test beds, first in line is the calibration team.

"They're the ones who do the whole engine strategy," Luzader says of the Roush group that handled the Terminator calibration engineering. "They map out the flow of engine emissions, cooling, heat protections, everything that has to do with the exhaust and meeting all of the federal standards. Basically, you can't drive the car unless they do their work."

This is just the beginning of the responsibilities of the calibrators, who then attend most tests after the various program aspects are underway.

"We've got those guys on-site with us when we're running tests," Luzader explains, "because if it's running too fat you're going to burn the cats up, if it's running too lean you'll burn the pistons up. They try to put a safe calibration in it to protect the cats and to protect the motor from leaning out. That's why the guys in the aftermarket can make so much power with this engine, because the calibration guys have put a relatively safe calibration in to make it live through all the durability tests."

The earliest prototype Terminators were the Workhorse Prototypes, "as crude of a prototype as you can get," notes Luzader. The 2001 Cobra loaded with engine compartment weights, used by the vehicle dynamics team to simulate the supercharged engine mass, was a Workhorse Prototype level vehicle.

Once specifics of the program were ready to be tested more formally, work began on the Attribute Prototypes.

"Those vehicles were built out of existing 2001 Cobras that we got out of Dearborn Assembly," reveals Luzader, "and then we basically put the powertrains in those cars – a real crude supercharged powertrain. I think we had probably fifteen of those cars for the life of the program in various stages that were used for calibration development, brake development, suspension development. So running around town you'd look at that car and it would look virtually no different than a 2001 Cobra."

As the pieces came together over the months of development, the Terminator began to take shape.

"Next we built our Confirmation Prototypes," Luzader says. "We built twelve of those: nine coupes and three convertibles. Those cars were built at Dearborn Assembly Plant on the assembly line, and that was really the first true Terminator-looking vehicle that came off the line.

"They had the flat black painted wheels and they had prototype body parts of the fascia and the hood," he continues. "But they were 'to program intent' – they weren't necessarily made out of the final production level materials. For example, the front fascias were made out of a prototype material to do it at a low cost. Because you don't want to spend the money to cut a full tool to do a production tool that early in the program."

The calibration team was hard at work through this whole period, chasing the ideal set-ups.

"It takes them about two to three months to fully instrument a car, to get all the wiring," Luzader explains. "Sometimes you'll see in development these big bundles of yellow wiring that they run through the car – that's for all the thermal couples and sensors. They mount sensors all along the exhaust and put temperature probes under the hood and basically fully instrument the car. So they don't necessarily want a new vehicle, because they'll lose that down time where they have to take the car apart and basically rebuild it."

Each stage reached by the calibrators made waves through all the prototype vehicles.

"Every time they get a new level of calibration, we go back and we update all the other vehicles," Luzader says of the fleet's on-board computer controls, "doing things like re-flashing the PCMs. So it's a never-ending process of updating the vehicles."

But with a growing number of prototypes being used to complete the stages of development, a rather obvious problem arose – how do you keep the project a secret?

Catch Me If You Can

From the beginning, SVT's Terminator had been a clandestine effort, one that was designed to surprise the automotive world upon its debut. Its existence was on a need-to-know basis.

"I was aware of the program early on," says Ford chairman Bill Ford. "Like every other Mustang fan, as soon as I heard about it I couldn't wait for it to be built."

Bill Ford's knowledge of the Terminator was to be expected. But interest in a factory supercharged Mustang or Cobra had always been extremely high among enthusiasts. Almost every year, rumors flew that such a model was about to debut. This time, the rumors were true.

One particular thorn in the team's side was the Internet site Blue Oval News (www.blueovalnews.com), a collection of often over-the-top discussion forums and breaking-news areas. From time to time, information that seemed to be coming from within Ford about various projects made its way to the Web site, and the Terminator program was no exception.

"They were getting a lot of insider information," says Primo Goffi. "There was a big push back then, as we wanted to keep everything really tight. A lot of things were getting out, especially on that site, as to what was going on in the company. There was a heightened level of sensitivity as to inside information getting on those Web sites."

Throughout 2001, the flow of information continued to appear. Although not always accurate – the site speculated that the Terminator was going to be a 2002 model sold as the "Cobra Special" – there were more than enough correct facts to aggravate SVT and excite Ford fans.

But even more exciting than words were images.

Confirmation Prototypes were beginning to venture out into the world. Brake testing contracted to LDW & Associates was underway, and one red coupe was sent to Los Angeles to run a city test. And even aftermarket companies that worked with SVT were being given a sneak peak of the new Cobra, to ensure the enthusiast buzz to "get even more power" would be at a fever pitch when the Terminator was released.

Though these prototypes hit the streets with camouflage panels of black vinyl attached to the vehicles with Velcro, it was hard to mistake the fact that this was no ordinary Mustang. The inevitable was about to happen.

A pastime in areas near automotive development centers is the capturing of "spy shots" – photos of cars under development. And when the vehicles are spotted and shot on public roads, there is nothing wrong with the practice – even if the auto manufacturers aren't very happy about it.

And so, on July 2, 2001, Nick Twork happened upon a Terminator prototype. Fortunately he had a camera at hand, and within days the auto world got its first clear look at the ominous visage of the new Cobra.

In Twork's hastily-snapped images, the Terminator sits at a traffic light in bright afternoon sunshine, a stealth-like, all-black vision caught on its short journey from the Dearborn Proving Grounds to the SVT/Roush complex. Sitting on specially-blackened trial wheels, menacing the sedate minivan next to it, the darkness of the vehicle's ample camouflage seems to absorb the very daylight. And the prototype's massive, high hood with dual vents hints broadly at the power that was still eight months from being officially unleashed.

Soon other pictures began to appear, including ones taken by the dean of spy photographers, Jim Dunne. Dunne captured for Popular Mechanics a silver prototype with powertrain engineer Jeff Grauer at the wheel, again on the hazardous trek from proving grounds to home base.

Occasionally a trespasser roaming the parking lot outside SVT's headquarters in Allen Park, Michigan would have a camera in hand – hence these two sets of spy shots. Obviously, focus was directed at the new design hallmarks that would come to characterize the Terminator, including its bulging hood and spoiler treatment.

These images were followed up by a series of poorly-lit, high-contrast photographs that appeared on the Blue Oval News site. They showed two Terminator prototypes, one silver and one black, parked in the rain outside the Roush/SVT complex. Though SVT contends that it is not legal for unauthorized personnel to traipse around its property, snapping photos of projects under development, multiple angles of the cars were posted, giving yet more proof that – despite the car's camouflage – something big was lurking under that complex hood.

Regardless of spies lurking in parking lots, at least some of the new Cobra sightings were authorized.

"Brian Roback was able to get a car out here," Brad Lammers says of a prototype's early debut for the workers at the Romeo Engine Plant Niche Line. "At the time it was in full 'camo,' with the body panels covered in canvas. He drove it right in through the back door, removed all the camouflage, and the guys got to see the car for the first time. Everybody was just ecstatic."

Late in the program, the builds evolved from Confirmation Prototypes to 1PPs – the first phase of Production Prove-out – and 4PPs, the Production Part Prove-out Program. The latter builds logically enough incorporate any changes necessitated from the 1PP builds. When this alphabet level was finally attained, the Terminator was production-ready.

"When we went to 1PP builds, we only built 4 of those," Luzader recalls, "and then as we got into the 4PP builds, there were a bunch built. But at that point our job is pretty much done. Those cars went to the marketing group, or over to Ford Customer Service Division so they could start doing labor time standards and shop manual stuff. So at that point it's populating the rest of the company with vehicles so they can start doing what they need to do, the last minute stuff."

Regardless of security concerns, the prototype levels that were built provided a concrete means for the Terminator team to measure their progress – without peering too far into the future.

"From a program standpoint, the end point is there, but you tend to set up these milestones in between," explains Tom Bochenek, the Terminator's program manager. "Once you build your Workhorse vehicle, then you've got something to work on. Then you've got AP prototypes and you build a couple more, and eventually you'll build some cars through the assembly plant.

"Every time you have an event," he continues, "it just triggers the whole system to provide cars, purchasing support, and all that. And you do that in phases – keep building and building and building until you finally get to the end. That's how you keep the momentum going. If you just sit there and look at the end? It's a long, long road…"

"How are we going to build a specialized performance vehicle on a standard production line?" That was the question that drove the building of a handful of production prototypes at Dearborn Assembly Plant. This later 4PP Terminator is being put together in secrecy on the line's night shift, its assembly offering proof that all production aspects – including installation of the unique front and rear fascia, the mating of the supercharged engine, and the implementation of the distinctive Terminator hood – had been fully addressed.

Photos: Tom Bochenek

CHAPTER 10

MUSCLE DOWN THE LINE

Building on History

Opposite: A Screaming Yellow Terminator convertible ends its journey through Dearborn Assembly Plant.
Photo: Marcie Cipriani

Above: Sprawling along the Rogue River, Ford Motor Company's massive operations reflect the peak of American industrial might in this image from 1927.
Photo: Ford Motor Company

While the Romeo Engine Plant's Niche Line had expanded, evolved, and adapted itself in fulfillment of its planned Terminator duties, such wholesale reinvention was an impossibility at the location where the new Cobra would be built – Ford's legendary Dearborn Assembly Plant, known simply as DAP.

DAP opened in 1918, initially christened "B Building" in its role as part of Ford's massive complex along the Rouge River south of Detroit. Aside from building passenger cars throughout its early decades of existence, the plant also assembled vast quantities of military vehicles – from boats to tanks – during war time. After creating Thunderbirds in the 1950s, DAP became the proud parent of Ford's famed Mustang upon that model's launch in 1964.

While the word "legendary" barely carries enough weight to convey the automotive history that has been made at this plant, in human characteristics DAP would best be described as old and cranky, set in its ways, and not inclined to quickly embrace change. In fact, any alteration to DAP processes had the potential to negatively impact production.

But change was exactly what the Terminator demanded, and communication between SVT and DAP began immediately upon program inception.

"After you have your PDL – the program direction letter – which basically lists the content of the program, you sit down with the plant and you walk through everything," says SVT's Nick Terzes. Assigned to vehicle operations for the team, Terzes' background with DAP manufacturing gave him clear perspective on the program challenges.

"You say, 'Look, here are the additional items that we're looking to do on the car,' and you start to get an idea of the effect it's going to have as far as complexity, and on any additional tooling that's going to be required.

"The plant's going to say certain things right off the bat – 'We just can't do this part,'" he continues, "and that's the first walkthrough. And then you go back with a revised list, and you start establishing what type of trials you need to do, what types of tooling changes will be required, and it's a matter of costing out...

"The Terminator was done on a very strict budget, considering the fact that we basically put an all-new powertrain and driveline in the car from a part number standpoint. The team did a great job, and I think the main reason is that they worked with the plant on a daily basis – they involved them every step of the way," Terzes concludes.

Opposite: The Ford Motor Company Rogue Plant complex at full production capacity, a maze of buildings, smokestacks, and connecting passageways.

Below: Scenes from four decades of Mustang production at the historic Dearborn Assembly Plant, the same efficient methodology followed from year to year. In the photo below right, under a banner that read "The Last Stampede," the final Mustang rolled off the DAP assembly line on May 10th, 2004. Soon after, Mustang production was moved approximately 30 miles south of Dearborn to the state-of-the-art Flat Rock Assembly Facility.

Photos: Ford Motor Company

THE LAST MUSTANG COBRA
BUILT AT THE DEARBORN ASSEMBLY PLANT

BY JIM SEISSER

The last Mustang Cobra built at the DAP, VIN 1FAFP49Y14F217149, a red convertible was assembled on March 31, 2004. We interviewed the owner of that historic car, Larry Plopan, a 34 1/2-year employee at the DAP about the Cobra and how he came about owning it.

MT: *Larry, how did it come about that you became the owner of the last Cobra built at Dearborn Assembly Plant?*

LP: I didn't set out with the goal to own the last Cobra from DAP—it just evolved. I've loved the look of the current Mustang since the 1999 style came out and I like the Cobra model the best. Every year since 1999 I kept thinking I needed to get one. Late last year I saw what the new 2005 Mustang was going to look like. It was nice, but I liked the looks of the current Mustang better so I went down to my dealership and put in an order for a new 2004 Cobra. I was able to get my order in before the Cobra orders were cut off. It's typical practice at most Ford assembly plants that the production of low-volume, specialty, or high-content vehicles get considered for build-out weeks before regular production ends. This makes the logistics easier for model-year change over in an assembly plant since there are fewer parts to change over all at one time. Since my car was ordered right at the end of Cobra production, I started thinking how I'd like mine to be the last DAP built Cobra. So I put the request in.

MT: *What is your position at the plant?*

LP: I'm in the shipping and receiving area. I'm the non-production stores supervisor.

MT: *What happens to Larry when the Dearborn Assembly closes, where you go?*

LP: I go over to the new truck plant next door.

MT: *What was it like to be able to watch your new car be built?*

LP: Our SVT group wanted to make an event out of this car getting built. So this car got a lot of attention and I got to watch it get built. Being the last Cobra, many of the workers on the line assumed this car was being built for some high-ranking executive. When I told them it was for me, some of the assembly workers on the line asked if they could sign it? Since it was my car I said sure why not? So on the underside of my car on the floor pan, while the car was being built, a lot of people signed my car. One guy signed my spare tire and one guy even signed the face of my front brake rotor. That signature disappeared the first time the brakes were applied. It was a lot of fun, but I found out later that it was a big no-no to let people sign a production car like that. I almost got in a lot of trouble over that.

MT: *You have a gorgeous red Cobra convertible, what do you plan on doing with it?*

LP: I plan to keep it; it's not for sale. I've had it for two months and it only has 200 miles on it. The weather has been really cold and I've only had the top down once since I've had it home. I plan on driving it, but plan on taking very good care of it. I don't plan on driving it in the winter. I have a daughter who lives in California. She has a 2002 Mustang GT coupe. She wants to know when I'm going to trade my Cobra convertible for her GT coupe? I told her she's not getting this one.

MT: *Did you watch your daughter's 2002 GT being built also?*

LP: No, she took one off the dealer's lot. She didn't want to wait.

MT: *How many Mustangs have you owned?*

LP: My wife and I had a dark blue 1965 coupe. I had a blue 1970 Mach 1. And I also had a 1986 Mercury Capri that was built at the Dearborn Assembly Plant.

MT: *What are you going to miss about the Dearborn Assembly Plant?*

LP: The closing of the plant is like the death of an empire. Most of us will be moving over to the new truck plant next door, but it's not the same. When we built the Mustang, it really was something special. We were the only plant building the Mustang so we got a lot of special attention that no other plant got. The new F150 is a beautiful vehicle and I know everyone will take great pride in building it. But when we build the new pickup truck we'll be one of three plants doing that. The Mustang was something that was special to everyone. *MT*

As the Dearborn Assembly Plant neared the end of its amazing run building Mustangs, a series of "lasts" made up the ending pages of the plant's history – and the final SVT Mustang Cobra to roll off the line was certainly a significant part of that tale.

Article courtesy Mustang Club of America.
Photos courtesy Dave Wagner

"I think a good part of SVT's success, especially with the '03 Cobra, revolves around relationship building and friendships that we've made in other areas of the company," acknowledges Primo Goffi. "I think Dearborn Assembly is a grand example. We developed a lot of friends like Al Frank and Tommy D – guys in there that are on board and want to make the car happen at least as much as we do. And without their help and their drive and their support and their dedication we'd have never made it."

SVT's "go to" guys at DAP were "Tommy D" Demeester and Al Frank. With literally decades of DAP experience between them, it seemed there was absolutely nothing they didn't know about Mustang assembly.

as manufacturing process engineer on the 2000 Cobra R program in 1998, so he had already faced the difficult task of making a niche vehicle fit within the standardized regimen at DAP.

"It was my primary responsibility to coordinate and communicate the engineering changes that we were making on the product to the plant," explains Diegel. "And my responsibility was to ensure the fact that the plant was ready to build the car. That went into organizing and coordinating all of the tooling changes that had to be made at the plant, holding weekly meetings to check out the status of where we were at, working with the suppliers to make sure they had clearance to come into the plant, scheduling the trials

Left: SVT's Nick Terzes (far left) played one of the most critical roles in the interaction between the high-performance engineering team and Dearborn Assembly Plant's Tommy Demeester (center) and Al Frank. This trio made sure Terminator assembly went off without a hitch.
Above: Dave Diegel had one of the most challenging tasks in the Terminator program: Assimilating a specialized performance vehicle into day-to-day assembly line productions.
Photos: Marcie Cipriani

"When we do a specialty car like the Cobra," Demeester says, "there's a whole lot of legwork on the outside. They have parts and bucks that we can go look at, but my biggest concern trying to bring it back in to the plant is looking at how it goes in, and then try to sequence everything."

Demeester and Frank interfaced daily with Dave Diegel, a man with decades of auto building program experience, including thirty-seven years at General Motors alone. Diegel was sought out by SVT to act

that we had to have at the plant, and making sure the plant was reimbursed for what had to happen."

A crucial component in the process of deciding how to build the Terminator was the use of a "design aid buck" – basically a prototype Cobra in the SVT/Roush garage that allowed engineers and DAP personnel the opportunity to study and theorize about the assembly of the vehicle.

"The design buck is something that you work on continuously," Diegel notes. "The main thing that you struggle with on the design buck is parts. We actually designed the intercooler system on the design aid buck."

"We'd take a part and we'd slap it on the car," recalls Demeester. "I'd take power tools over and zip it up, say, 'OK this is what we have to do,' then collectively sit down and we'd write a process on how to do it way before we went into production."

Demeester and Frank were often accompanied by the operators who would actually be doing the assembly of a part or component under review.

"We've had training sessions where I've taken the operators over to Roush to work on the cars there with me," Demeester acknowledges.

"I'd grab those operators and take them over there and say, 'Listen, you're going to be doing this' – to get their input. They're going to have to be installing it all the time, so I let them fool with it and they might see something that we wouldn't even think of looking at."

One of the major Terminator issues, though, was something beyond the scope of the buck studies. The larger 275 Goodyear tire that the vehicle dynamics team had fought so hard for caused massive ripples throughout the Tire Line assemblies. Trial after trail was held in the middle of the night or whenever time could be stolen in the busy plant, resulting in changes to angle iron where the tires and wheels were mated, alterations in tire filling, and the introduction of special plastic mounting sockets to avoid wheel scratches. Even the conveyors that slide the tire/wheel assemblies toward the vehicles all had to be raised to accommodate the new tires.

A dizzying inventory of wheels and tires were brought together and then automatically transported along mechanical conveyance deep within Dearborn Assembly Plant, each pairing precisely timed to arrive on the line for mounting on the Mustang they were destined to serve.
Photos: Marcie Cipriani

The new TREMEC six-speed transmission also created its own DAP headaches.

"One of the first things that we ran into there was the fact that our transmission interfered with the current underbody," reveals Diegel. "So, we had to cut out a section of the tunnel. We had to use a plasma cutter, and we had to get Dearborn to agree to do that where they do the match check for the underbody. The underbody comes across and a tag notes, this is a Cobra – so then that car had to have this center section cut out with the plasma."

A myriad of smaller changes caused their own ripples through the system. The Terminator's unique front and rear springs specific to coupe or convertible, unique rocker panels, specialized side scoop inserts, unique side view mirrors – these items all took up valuable floor space in cramped areas of the plant. But uniformity despite the uniqueness was crucial – the racks holding six Terminator front fascia had the same footprint as racks holding eight regular Mustang fascia, to allow standardization of inventory movement and storage.

"Those are the kinds of things that don't have anything to do with the tooling, they don't have anything to do with the way the car goes together, but you have to plan them into the process," stresses Diegel. "And that all has to be talked about with the plant up front. You have to be honest and let them know as soon as you become aware of whatever is changing on your product so they can start making their changes."

Many aspects of the new Cobra required improvisation, such as the decision to route the supercharger's boost gauge vacuum line alongside the heater core en route to the instrument panel. But sometimes the Terminator demanded changes to the actual assembly equipment and related procedures.

"You decide to do it – OK, that's one thing," says Cobra program manager Tom Bochenek. "Then figuring out how to get all the components, get them built, go through the assembly process – that was just relentless. Every weekend at Dearborn Assembly, and during the week, just trying to get the thing to deck…

"For example, there's an arm that comes down and grabs the hood and opens it as it starts down the chassis line," he continues. "That

all had to be redone for the hood – not a trivial thing. What we did was we built a prototype through the system, identified all of the areas that we thought we'd have issues with, then we had to develop plans to go fix all of them with the vehicle operations people. Then, on the other side, make sure the engineering is there to handle it with timing."

"On the hood lift mechanism the suction cups were hitting where the air extractors were," Dave Diegel says of the new Cobra's hood. "And not only that, but the weight of that hood, versus the weight of the other hoods, was different. So it all had to be recalibrated. We were in there two or three weekends just getting the design modified for that hood lift equipment."

Then there was the matter of the supercharger's intercooler, a combination of plumbing, pumps, and coolant reservoirs that no other Mustang had. It was a totally new vehicle system for DAP to deal with – and a major disruption.

"It's a totally independent fluid system that required us to install an entirely separate fluid fill," says SVT's Nick Terzes. "It had a lot of components in a very tight engine compartment, and you've got all these areas where there is leak potential."

Studying the design aid buck, the team came up with a solution that would require a new assembly area in DAP.

"With the intercooler, we wrote that process, added manpower for that job, designed a work table and had it built," Tommy Demeester says. "We had a rough idea of what we wanted, and we took it over to the supplier and said, 'OK, here's our part. We want a table that we can put this in to build it up and clamp it all up with spots for all the shelves and stuff.'"

Dave Diegel recalls spending weekend after weekend at DAP, honing the development and calibration of the mechanism to fill the new intercooler before an accurate system was in place for production.

The intercooler itself is just one engine component, and "decking the engine" – loading the massive, 655-pound assembly into the vehicle – was one of the most critical and dangerous aspects of building the Terminator at DAP.

"To me, that's not a job that I'd want to do," avers SVT powertrain engineer Dave Dempster. "These guys that deck the engine over there? I see those guys ramming the engines up in there, and their hands are right up in there, pulling that steering shaft…"

"They were sending me engines with superchargers and the new transmissions over here from the shop on wood pallets so I could make all the modifications, like changing all the chains on the engine line," Tommy Demeester says. "So it was at least a good year before we went into production when I was doing all the trials for the engine hanging and stuffing the engine."

The planning with DAP naturally involved give and take on various aspects of the Terminator program. SVT's Scott Tate had hoped to add some of his driver seat features to the passenger seat. But the seat electronics would have demanded a unique interior carpet set in an area where assembly line space is critical, so DAP said no. On the other hand, a pinch flange cut out requested by Mark Dipko's chassis team, to accommodate the 275 tires, was agreeable to DAP – and by necessity for uniform assembly, thereafter was included in all production Mustangs.

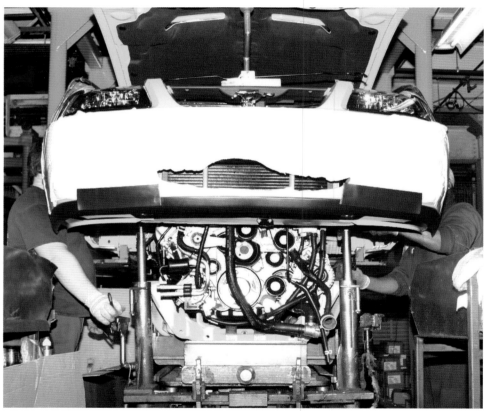

One of the most intimidating aspects of life on the Dearborn Assembly Plant line: the painstaking process of mating the massive, supercharged engine from the Romeo Engine Niche Line with the Mustang Cobra that would rely on its power.
Photo: Marcie Cipraini

Under Cover of Night

The planning carried out by SVT and DAP was so efficient, and the parties worked so well together, that the new Cobra's Confirmation Prototypes were built along the line as an early test.

"We did our CP build in the plant," Nick Terzes reveals, "and a lot of times you wouldn't necessarily do it in the plant. You'd do it either off-site or at a pilot plant. But this was our opportunity to build a handful of cars ahead of time, on the line, to trial everything out."

The CP builds were largely successful, so it was with an air of confidence that the teams moved on toward the near-production prototype builds of the 1PP and 4PP cars.

"The 1PP build is a nonsaleable car," Terzes says, "but you'll build it right on the assembly line, you'll follow all the procedures, and if you find a problem you'll document it, you'll make it a design change or a process change if it's required… Before the next build you might trial it if you can, without necessarily having the Cobra on the line. Then you go to your next build and try it again, and hopefully you've fixed all your issues."

These latter prototypes are typically built at night, unlike the early test vehicles. If one of these builds was underway when the plant shut down in the early morning hours, the prototype build team had no choice but to wait around until production resumed with the next shift.

"We do most of our early prototype work all on day shift because it's convenient for everyone," Tommy Demeester says. "But prior to production, we have to run those cars at night. So we'll tell everyone, 'We're going to run five Cobras on the night shift.' And if we don't get them off line…

"If those cars are still in the system at three in the morning, well guess what?" Demeester asks. "We're going to have to stay here until the line starts up in the morning. Everybody looks at each other and says, 'What are you talking about?' Well, what are we going to do – just take off and leave nobody here with the cars? So it could wind up being a very long day, and we've had plenty of those."

The concept of such dedication became a reality only because of the mutual respect between SVT and the DAP workers.

2003 MY
COBRA
4PP BUILD
Build it right the first time

"I was always in engineering from the earliest parts of my career," Dave Diegel says. "So I found out that engineering was very reluctant to work with the plant – the engineers always thought they knew more and that they knew better, and that they didn't have to go to the plant. It was a, 'We design the car, you build it,' kind of thing. That mentality doesn't exist over here – it's hand in hand."

"We have the utmost respect for those guys, and I think they have it for us, too," Tommy Demeester says earnestly. "They know what our job entails over here at the plant, trying to coordinate everything with the prototype parts that come in. And I know what those guys go through, trying to get something like that off the ground."

"The enthusiasm level, and the friendship between the plant and the SVT team – they wanted to make this car happen quickly," says Nick Terzes, who's seen the relationship from both perspectives. "They knew the timing, the plant was very cognizant of how quickly this car had to launch and they went out of their way to make sure it happened. It was, 'Can do! We have to make it happen.' And that's why you were able to compress and do a program that would normally take thirty to forty percent longer."

"The passion of the Dearborn Assembly Plant was by far one of our enablers," SVT's Celeste Kupczewski states. "If we didn't have that… At Dearborn, they had the Mustang history and the passion for the product: 'Oh my god, we're finally going to make a 400-horsepower Mustang? There's no way in hell we're not going to make this happen!'"

CHAPTER 11 POWER TO THE PEOPLE

Perception Becomes Reality

Ford's Special Vehicle Team inhabits a low, modern office complex owned by Roush Industries, located off Rotunda Drive near Dearborn. In fact, if it wasn't for an unusual-looking vehicle here and there, and evidence that someone's been doing burnouts in the parking lot, the facility would not look out of place in Mike Judge's movie parody of corporate life, *Office Space*.

SVT occupies one of two buildings, joined in the center by a large garage area. Here the clandestine automotive operations of the team and Roush are carried out, with the latter company set up in the northern building.

In SVT's space, John Coletti's office overlooks the parking lot and anchors the engineering section and its conference and meeting rooms. Sandwiched between engineering and the garage facility are SVT's business operations offices. Here Bob Lewis oversees the dealer affair concerns, and the marketing and communications group handles their efforts, including answering the numerous consumer calls that come in to the SVT Information Center's 800-FORDSVT hot line.

And speaking of calls, it's also here that Alan Hall sat in his office throughout 2001, fielding query after query from the media, all demanding information about one thing: "What's this I hear about a supercharged Cobra?" Particularly after the publication of spy photos mid-year, the cat was definitely clawing its way out of the bag. But in his job as communications manager for SVT, Hall remained in a professional state of denial.

"I think we were all relieved because we knew it was going to be a great car. I wanted to be able to tell people, but you couldn't," Hall says of the persistent media queries. "Rumors get out, and with the Internet and things like that, the truth got out in the rumors, but I had to fight them off."

The new Cobra was a magnet for such speculation.

"Of any car that we have, the Cobra has the most rumors and interest," Hall acknowledges. "We get calls on the info center all the time, and some of the stuff that people call us about is unbelievable, that they hear. 'I hear it's coming with nitrous – is that true?' All kinds of crazy stuff."

Equally crazy, though, were some of the attempts at deception made by Hall and his cohorts, trying to send the media off on the wrong trail even after spy photos of the Terminator began to appear. SVT's official party line was to act mystified when supercharger questions arose.

"In those photos you can see the air extractors on the hood, so sometimes the camouflage plays into pointing out areas of unique bits," Hall says. "There were also A-pillar gauges visible – boost gauges – and you could obviously see them right through the window. That was the biggest giveaway. People said, 'Man, that has a boost gauge – why would you

Above: At a media event at the Chicago Auto Show on February 6, 1992, Ford announced the creation of a new high performance division, the Special Vehicle Team, and presented their first two public offerings, the 1993 SVT F-150 Lightning and the 1993 SVT Mustang Cobra. It was only fitting that the same venue be chosen for the unveiling of the Terminator in 2002.

Photo courtesy John Clor

Right: The parking lot outside the unassuming building that houses the SVT offices shows definite evidence of "improvised acceleration testing."

Photo: Marcie Cipriani

have a boost gauge?' 'Well, it's actually not a boost gauge, it's measuring oil pressure' or something. But we just couldn't get out of that one."

Eventually, SVT began to play things up with the project's code name, allowing the supercharger rumors to bolster the shadowy image of the new vehicle.

"We tried to play that up," admits Hall, "and use 'Terminator' to kind of foreshadow the belief that this would end all worries or concerns over, 'Does the Cobra have enough power? Will it be able to compete?' It was just the end of all those discussions – terminate all the discussions, it's done, this is the 'end all, be all' product."

The Terminator's public unveiling would end the secrecy once and for all, and SVT's plans for this event were focused on the 2002 edition of one of the world's great displays of new automobiles, the Chicago Auto Show.

"At least with a year out you're pretty much confirmed as to what show you have," Hall reveals. "Because it's not just up to me to pick the show – obviously I've got to take it and fit it in with the rest of what Ford Motor Company is doing. So that decision is pretty much made a year out and locked in. We always look for Chicago first because that's our show, where SVT was originally announced back in 1992."

The Show Goes On

By January, 2002, as the Chicago Auto Show's opening in February neared, speculation about the Cobra had reach a fevered pitch.

But no more fevered than the atmosphere at the Dearborn Assembly Plant. On January 23, just two weeks before the show was to begin, four 1PP prototypes were built. These were the Terminators destined to be the first officially shown to the world. Three coupes and one convertible made their way down the line, anxiously attended to by the build team.

Early in the first week of February, two of these new builds – a red convertible and a blue coupe – were packed up in the cold Michigan air, bound for Chicago's show, scheduled to open on February 8. But that was just the official date to debut the car; in reality, privileged eyes in Illinois were popping at the sight of the supercharged Mustang in the days leading up to the "public reveal."

On Tuesday, February 5, a mysterious, fully-covered car arrived in the showroom of the largest volume Ford dealer in Illinois. A group of excited people crowded around the hidden vehicle in the Arlington Heights Ford showroom, until 7:02 p.m. At that moment, SVT marketing director Tom Scarpello threw back the cover, and a cluster of SVT Owners Association guests saw the Terminator with their own eyes. The red convertible nearly elicited a collective swoon among the diehard SVT fans, who had traveled from as far away as Alaska to attend the event.

Photos from this early reveal began to ricochet around the Internet within hours, and one interested observer was Brad Lammers, the Terminator's manufacturing engineer at Romeo Engine Plant.

Scenes from a revelation. It's just after 7PM on February 5, 2002, and a group of guests invited to Arlington Heights Ford are among the first members of the public to get a good long look at a Terminator production prototype.

As part of the engine manufacturing verification process, Lammers and SVT's Brian Roback had attempted to build an engine on the Niche Line, just as the two-man teams would do in production.

"Brian and I built an engine and we tried to do it within the line cycle time," Lammers laughs. "We didn't do it. In fact, there were several times where the operators were kind of razzing us: 'Come on guys, hurry up – we do this in six-and-a-half minutes, why can't you guys get it done?'"

Being without a signature plate like those attached to engines built by the Niche Line teams, Lammers and Roback signed their engine with a bold blue marker. Months later, on the evening of the advance reveal at the Ford dealership, Lammers got a call.

"My buddy said, 'I just saw an article on the Cobra,'" Lammers recalls, "so I checked it out on-line. There were pictures from all around the car, with one of the hood open. And right there, you can see the paint from the blue marker where Brian and I signed the engine. We had no idea! We thought it was just going to be a dyno engine… To see it on-line, with all those people looking at it – what a cool feeling!"

The next day, Ford employees had their own Terminator sneak peek on-site at the Chicago Auto Show, an event that led up to Ford's media press conference on February 7.

That morning, the Chicago Auto Show Web site did a favor for Ford fans around the world by providing Web-cam access to the events about to unfold.

Shortly after 11 a.m. local time, the air was split by the composite sound of rumbling exhaust and supercharger whine. Before the wondering eyes of the assembled media, John Coletti and Tom Scarpello careened into the presentation behind the wheel of the blue Terminator coupe, their burnout trailed by a cloud of smoke.

The members of SVT would not have had it any other way.

"As both a business person and a Mustang fan my reaction was the same – this is great!" Ford chairman and chief executive officer Bill Ford says of the Terminator's debut. "But I wasn't surprised at all. I knew it would be a big hit."

The now-infamous 'carpet burnout' performed by Tom Scarpello at the 2002 Chicago Auto Show quickly made its way around the internet, much to the delight of Ford fans around the world.
Photos: Ford Motor Company

The Terminator had been seen by the world, and the excitement evident in the crowds of people who thronged around the two Cobras until the Chicago Auto Show closed on February 17 offered visceral proof that SVT had lit a passionate fuse among performance auto fans. Surely the project pace could ease off a touch after sixteen months of flat-out development, couldn't it?

No. In Michigan, Mike Luzader was preparing for the next – and final – round of prototypes to be build at Dearborn Assembly. In New Jersey, Michael Tokarchik was honing his manufacturing plan as Manley Performance Products prepared to step up to the level of OEM supplier. In Arizona, details were confirmed for the SVT vehicle dynamics team to run their final eight-hour durability test.

The smoke clears at the 2002 Chicago Auto Show and SVT's boss John Coletti strides to the podium – but the shocking entrance that he and Tom Scarpello had just made in a roaring, wide-open-throttle Terminator had already made SVT's point abundantly clear.
Photos: Ford Motor Company

If anything, the pace was quickening, all in pursuit of the new Cobra's first day of production: Job One, scheduled for early May. That date was closing in fast.

Speaking of the February 5 Terminator "sneak peak" for members of the SVT Owners Association, SVT's Celeste Kupczewski says, "I think that was a night we all looked at each other and said, 'Well, we've got to do it now!' Now it's real."

Alan Hall certainly felt the pressure. Though the Terminator had been revealed, Hall's real job was just getting underway. To make the most of the new Cobra's news potential, Hall had to coordinate an intricate series of appearances, all designed to maximize the coverage that the car would receive in media outlets.

The automotive press receive varying levels of access to new vehicles based on program status. Sometimes it's a drive, where they are allowed to try out a model under controlled conditions, while other times they are loaned a vehicle for more in-depth exploration.

The new Cobra coverage began with a mere look-over for *Motor Trend*, who received no drive time whatsoever while shooting photography of an early red convertible in November, 2001. But this was more than enough to generate a cover story in the March, 2002 issue, under a bold headline proclaiming, "Power of the Future."

"We were able to do a pre-story," Hall says of the Terminator's first cover. "This came out in February of 2002, and was a pre-placed story to hit the same month as the Chicago Auto Show, an exclusive cover story with *Motor Trend*. And that wasn't a drive, it was just a reveal, introducing the car."

But the uproar from the auto media was growing. Some had seen an early prototype at a December 11, 2001 media gathering to review all upcoming Ford products. But that presentation was "embargoed," an agreement under which the publications keep quiet about what they have seen until given the go-ahead to proceed with stories. Still others had been allowed to do their own limited photography shortly after the initial *Motor Trend* session.

But all of the magazines were clamoring for seat time in the Terminator. Described as "long lead time" outlets – since weeks usually pass between an article submission and publication – the magazines presented Hall with a challenge: how to set up drives so the issues would hit the newsstands and arrive in mailboxes just as the new Cobra began to appear in showrooms. Hall managed to work out an arrangement with the vehicle dynamics team, who were planning to begin their second eight-hour test on February 27 at Firebird International Raceway near Phoenix.

"The Phoenix car was a 1PP level car, when we did our eight-hour test which served as part of our final engineering sign-off," says SVT's Mike Luzader. "We also did a final engineering sign-off drive out there at the same time; we had a whole other group of guys doing engineering sign-off on the other 1PP vehicles.

"And then the next day, after two days worth of eight-hour testing, we moved over to one of the other tracks out there and we did the long-lead media drive," he continues. "We brought journalists in and they got into the same eight-hour car, with the telemetry still on it. Half of them did the morning at the track while the other half had the two engineering sign-off cars – production type level cars – and they went out and tooled around the mountains and back roads out there."

Pre-production units doubled as media drive cars following grueling eight-hour test days at Firebird International Raceway near Phoenix.

How did the media react to the car? Alan Hall quickly recites a roster of cover stories about the Terminator.

"We already had *Motor Trend*, then we got *AutoWeek*. *Sports Car International* drove it later but they gave us a cover story. *Muscle Mustangs and Fast Fords* and *5.0 Mustang*. *Car and Driver*, we got that story, another cover," he notes. "To us, that's the pinnacle of success in the media, that it's cover worthy. But that's what SVT's job is to do at Ford Motor Company – to cast this performance halo at Ford Motor Company. If these cars can not get on the cover of magazines, then we're doing something wrong."

There was indeed a heady glow of near-ecstatic media coverage – although to designer Camilo Pardo's slight dismay, the focus continually dwelled on the Terminator's most obvious attribute, its power. Pardo had effectively rejuvenated and cleaned up an iconic-but-tired automotive visage, yet the Cobra's menacing new look went almost unnoticed in print.

"As far as design, we didn't get much exposure from this car," Pardo admits. "All the magazines came out and they didn't say a thing – they were all just discussing the horsepower, which is very important, but man…"

If there were Terminator aspects that drew criticism, it was that the foundation of the car was over twenty years old, and that some new, hi-tech advancements had passed by SVT's flagship vehicle.

But SVT's engineers are familiar with those charges, and many feel that the Terminator's no-frills, high-performance attitude was exactly what was needed.

"Do we really think the Cobra buyer cares that he doesn't have a heads-up electronic display, like a Corvette owner might want? I don't think so," concludes powertrain engineer Dave Dempster. "You want to be able to see the boost gauge, you want to be able to shift it, you want to be

The automotive media reaction to the Terminator was nearly unanimous in its praise for the car's power and handling.
Photo: Frank Moriarty

able to steer it – keep the sensory inputs, but forget about the lighted door switches and the lighted vanity mirrors."

"You see these media guys get in there and they do that, they pick on that kind of stuff," agrees fellow powertrain engineer Brian Roback. "Yes, some of that stuff's a little outdated, but it's an older model car that's been refined over the years. So they do that kind of stuff – and then they go drive it. They come out with a big smile on their face. 'So did you have fun?' 'Oh, God yeah! That was fun!' And that's our point right there. That's what we're trying to get."

Name Check

To the media covering this latest development from SVT, the story was clear: this was a brand new, extremely powerful Cobra. But in the minds of many of the new vehicle's own suppliers, there was a bit of confusion. Yes, there was a new Cobra – but what about that Terminator?

As production neared, the decision had been made to leave the code name "Terminator" behind due to concerns over both licensing with the Hollywood crowd and the fact that the name could be considered a little too aggressive to represent product from a major American auto manufacturer.

But some people continued to believe they were working on a car called Terminator.

"We confused everybody outside and inside the company," program manager Tom Bochenek concedes. "They actually thought there was another model coming out beside the Cobra."

"We were going to production prototypes six months before Job One and there were still suppliers who didn't know 'Terminator' was a Cobra," Celeste Kupczewski laughs. "We got to the point where we were past public introduction, and we were not allowed to use the Terminator nomenclature. So we were calling suppliers and saying, 'I need my Cobra drawings,' and they were saying, 'We don't work on Cobra!'"

Eventually, the confusion was cleared up, and all parts associated with the new Cobra were cleared of the project name – except one.

"The back of the grille on the quarter panel scoop has 'Terminator,'" reveals Kupczewski. "They weren't actually supposed to put that in… It was just an internal thing. And then, the next thing we know, we get this part that says 'Terminator' on the back!"

By that point, it was too late to make any changes. At long last, production was ready to begin.

The only part on the 2003-2004 SVT Mustang Cobra bearing the name "Terminator" is this side air scoop insert.
Photo: Frank Moriarty

The Hands of Craftsmen

In April, 2002, the Niche Line at Romeo Engine Plant began to build the first Cobra engines destined for vehicles that would soon be on sale in Ford's SVT dealerships.

The Niche Line had undergone more than a mere physical expansion to allow the complete assembly of engines from start to finish. To make use of all the line station space and maintain the build cycle times, the number of two-man teams was doubled to twenty.

"The experienced people who had been here for a few years, they were excited to get going on it, and they had been involved in the pre-production builds and things like that," says Niche Line coordinator Cary Kramp. "So we actually split those teams up and had them work with the new guys who came out for up-manning the line. They helped me train all the new people who came out."

Terminator production began along the Niche Line each day at 5 a.m., the operators arriving in the pre-dawn darkness and either picking up where they left off the previous day or starting a new engine.

Each Terminator powerplant entered the Niche Line as a block. Its journey began at the first of the new expansion stations built on the north side of the line, before moving slowly from station to station in a counter-clockwise direction, its pace set according to uniform cycle time automation. With its two-man build team following each engine on its oval, racetrack-shaped expedition, the circuit entailed a two-hour-plus lap that saw each assembly built up from bare components to finished engine.

By the time an engine passed through turns one and two of an assembly lap, the crankshaft and piston assemblies had been precisely located. Nearing turn three, the engine was largely built and the cold test machine ensured the engine was tight. It was also here that the Ford SVT/UAW engine team signature plate was added. At the exit of turn four the final assemblies were added, and upon crossing the finish line the new engine was hoisted from its cradle on the line, ready for final inspection and migration to the Dearborn Assembly Plant.

A giant stereo boom box, paid for and shared by the operators, accompanied the teams' efforts with a wildly diverse array of music

Ron Anderson (left) and Bob McIntyre (right) made up one of the elite two-man teams who carefully hand-assembled every Terminator engine on the Niche Line. The quality and consistency of the line is exceptional.
Photo: Frank Moriarty

each day, from old-school country to thunderous hard rock. But that wasn't the only engine-building soundtrack: to signal the graduation of each engine to production status, one team member rang a brass bell to announce completion of every assembly lap.

"Our best day ever was with nineteen teams," Cary Kramp says, "and we built sixty-seven engines. On average we were building fifty-five to sixty engines a day."

Tom Wilson, Romeo Engine's manufacturing engineer lead, marvels over the Niche Line efforts, noting, "In a day when automation is the prime direction in a lot of assembly processes, to have an engine that's almost one hundred per cent hand assembled, with operator responsibility, and to have the quality that these guys have…"

"Hand building engines isn't something that's done much in this modern day and age," agrees Terminator engineer lead Brad Lammers. "From a bottom line, big picture perspective, there's probably what might be viewed as a lot of waste in a hand-built process. But you know, SVT contacts us regularly because customers want extra signature plates – they love the fact that this car is hand built. And you don't see that except in the $300,000 cars. Those are the ones that are hand built. It's just not done."

Under Production

When the first new Cobra engines arrived at the Dearborn Assembly Plant, nearly forty miles to the south of Romeo Engine Plant, months of preparation had paid off: all was in readiness to build Terminators.

On May 8, 2002, the workers at DAP completed Job One: the first 2003 SVT Mustang Cobra ready for sale. This Cobra – and all that would come in its wake – followed a serpentine assembly path that stretched nine miles within the maze-like confines of the historic facilities first built by Henry Ford on the banks of the Rouge River. On its trek, the Terminator quickly evolved from bare sheet metal to finished vehicle.

The basic shape of each Cobra, like that of all Mustangs, was stamped from metal, then formed into a sub-assembly. Once all the body panels were securely welded in place, the framework was sent through the painting facility. Mounted on a sled that would bear the Cobra for much of its manufacturing journey, the painted skeleton entered a towering, multi-tiered storage facility, where the body would slumber until a speeding robot assembly plucked it from its bay to begin the final assembly journey.

Once "dropped" into the final DAP process, Cobras began a remarkable transformation in their final seven hours of construction. While the bodies entered one line section, in another location the engines took up residence on a conveyor, as the wheels and tires were mounted in yet another area. Each component was timed and scheduled to meet up with its Cobra host, all at the right time and place in the assembly process.

Top: John Coletti, Tom Bochenek and plant manager Mark Boldin stand with the first 2003 Terminator to be built at DAP.
Photo: Tom Bochenek

Bottom: Deep within Dearborn Assembly Plant, thousands upon thousands of horsepower await their call to Mustang Cobra duty.
Photo: Marcie Cipriani

Working in DAP was like laboring in a panorama of perpetual motion, with tugs and forklifts ferrying in supplies as they raced through the gloom on timbers dating back to the plant's very origins decades before. Robots spun and swung as they completed an endless array of precise tasks, while everywhere in sight components relentlessly moved forward on their automated journeys.

As each Terminator moved down the line, dashboards and seats were added, electrical assemblies were put in place, the freshly-assembled supercharger intercooler was mounted, the special front fascia was attached, the body and chassis assembly was decked with the engine, the independent rear suspension was rammed into place, custom rocker panels were installed, the wheel and tire assemblies were mounted – all accomplished at a never-slowing pace. It was a staggering feat of logistical planning, fully realized in a near-seamless procedure, and no less impressive in light of the fact that such complexity characterizes all modern automobile assembly processes.

By the time a Terminator rolled off the line – crossing the very same "finish line" that Mustangs had passed over since 1964 – the vehicle was ready for final inspection, preparation, and transportation to the selling dealership that had ordered the car.

That the workers at DAP could accommodate the building of the Terminator – a vehicle that demanded so many exceptional assembly steps – while not disrupting the one-Mustang-every-ninety-seconds pace of the line stands as a testament to both their skills and their pride in the fact that they were the most crucial component in the realization of SVT's high performance visions.

"We had a good plan, with everything working in parallel, and you need to do that in order to get all the tasks done in time," says Cobra program manager Tom Bochenek. "But the manufacturing guys in Dearborn? Oh, they were great! They bent over backwards. We had done the Cobra R over there, so they were ready for another one."

"It's the big thing," DAP's Tommy Demeester says of the workers who built the Cobras. "They love it. They get zipped up about it out here at the plant, because we get to build some real exciting vehicles."

Left: Painted bodies in storage, soon to be sent down the assembly line and built into one of several versions of the Mustang. Right: A 2004 Terminator begins to take shape. More photos of the assembly process can be found in the Appendix.
Photos: Marcie Cipriani

A Record Breaking Bargain

No doubt, the 2003 SVT Mustang Cobra was an exciting vehicle. It was largely hand-built, with ample capacity to multiply its imposing horsepower at the hands of owners via simple modifications. But there was one other equally impressive aspect of the Terminator: with a base list price just over $33,000 for the coupe and $5000 more for the convertible, it was an undeniable bargain.

"What we were trying to accomplish was to establish it as a unique proposition in the marketplace, and it is," states Tom Scarpello, the SVT marketing head who worked with John Coletti to shepherd the car to production. "There's nothing else you can buy with that kind of performance, that kind of power, for that price – it's just out there on its own, and that's what we were trying to do."

"I think the fact that it runs a 12.90 quarter mile at 113, 112 miles per hour – that kind of answers itself," notes Tom Chapman, chassis systems supervisor. "This car is fast, period."

"After having a lot of conversations about what kind of car is out there to compete with the Cobra, the first name that comes to mind from just about everybody is the Corvette," notes Cary Kramp. "Well, we've proved over the last two years that a standard C5 Corvette is no match for us. That's within the same price range. The Z06 – yes, we can hang with the Z06, but the Z06 on average is over $15,000 more than the Cobra, so where's the comparison?"

"I can tell you for sure there's nothing under $60,000 that even comes close to it," John Coletti firmly states, "and you can probably crank it up to $70,000 – then you're getting close to a Viper kind of price. But for the value?"

Coletti speculates that the cost for a user to upgrade a 2001 Cobra to the level of the Terminator – rebuilding the engine with competition-quality components, adding an Eaton supercharger, improving the independent rear suspension – would be substantially over $10,000, not to mention the voiding of the factory warranty. Yet SVT raised the price of the 2003 Cobra by under $5000 to cover those parts enhancements and the thousands of hours of engineering work the Terminator demanded.

Perhaps the greatest compliment to the new Cobra came with the June 2003 issue of *Motor Trend* magazine, when the Terminator was chosen for a high-performance shootout. It's competition included not only big-ticket domestic competitors like the Dodge Viper SRT-10 ($83,795) but also foreign supercars like the Ferrari 575M Maranello ($241,092) and the Lamborghini Murcielago ($284,850).

It's little wonder that buyers immediately responded to the value of the Terminator.

"The customer reaction was tremendous," states long-time SVT dealer Darin Kreiss. "Two of the first cars we sold were commitments by people who bought the cars before they saw them. After that, we had a waiting list of people. Everybody was really excited. The magazines had done some tremendous articles on the car, and the hype around the car was just huge. So we didn't have any problem selling that product for an entire year."

This reception came as a relief to the dealers, following what amounted to a season of doubt. When it was announced that there would be no 2002 Cobra, the dealers were upset they had no new Cobra to sell – and concerned about the future.

"My initial reaction was one of concern that the Cobra program may be dying," recalls Kreiss. "The Cobra was somewhat stale by that point. With just having come off of the horsepower issue from '99, no Cobra for 2000, limited interest for 2001 and now no 2002 Cobra, the future for the car looked bleak.

"Even with these issues there was still huge customer interest in the Cobra, but they wanted something new and exciting," he continues. "Since 1996 when the Cobra got the four-valve motor it only received minimal changes to the cosmetics, suspension and horsepower. These improvements weren't enough."

When word got out that the reason the 2002 model had been cancelled was to create a Cobra with new levels of power, "it created a new buzz about the car," Kreiss says. "That was enough to keep those customers on the edge of their seats waiting for word on what 2003 would hold for the Cobra."

Right:
Darin Kreiss of Maguire's Ford Duncannon, PA.
Photo: Frank Moriarty
Opposite:
2004 Cobra in Competition Orange posing in front of Ford World Headquarters in Dearbon, Michigan.
Photo: Jeff Perlaky

In 2003 and 2004, John Maffucci set land speed records of 176.516 and 203.231 mph respectively –remarkable considering he was at the wheel of a largely stock Terminator.

Photos courtesy John Maffucci

In fact, Kreiss was so impressed with the Terminator that he not only sold them, he bought one himself.

"I loved the look of it," he enthuses. "I like the aggressive look of the bulging hood, the way that they re-contoured the lower valance on the front of the car – it really gave it a mean look. It's a very aggressive looking car."

But there was an additional audience who recognized the value of the new Cobra for far more than mere street use. This vehicle easily served as a perfect platform for racing development, and within months of the Terminator's appearance in showrooms in June 2002, the model began to make its presence felt on America's racetracks.

In the world of drag racing, "Nitrous Pete" Misinsky, using the short block of the 2003 Cobra in its stock configuration, early on tweaked his Terminator to approach 700 horsepower with speeds at 140 mph in the quarter-mile, with fellow New Jersey drag racer Jim D'Amore finding equal success in his own Cobra. Soon numerous drivers were pushing their modified Cobras into 9-second strip passes.

In road racing, competition in the Grand-Am Cup Series was enlivened by the Terminator of Shreiner Racing, which made its presence felt in events at famous tracks like Watkins Glen International.

But perhaps the most unusual claim to fame staked by the new Cobra came on the historic salt flats of Bonneville, Utah, where each year hundreds of drivers attempt to set new world land speed records.

Astonishingly, John Maffucci drove his nearly stock 2003 Cobra from Dawsonville, GA to Bonneville, where on August 18, 2003 he set a new C/PS record of 176.516 mph. He then turned around and drove the car back home to Georgia.

Returning a year later, on August 16, 2004, Maffucci re-set his class record, with a historic blast of 203.231 mph. Somewhere, John Coletti smiled.

Reaping the Rewards

In just eighteen intense months, the Cobra had undergone a light-speed evolution, from a naturally aspirated vehicle that drew John Coletti's unbridled wrath to Ford Motor Company's high-powered star of magazine covers.

"That's what these programs are all about: short fused, short timing, low resources. They're full of some monumental challenges," says Cobra team manager Primo Goffi. "Some people thrive on them, some people don't. So we'd like to think… Call us crazy, call us what you want, but we wouldn't have it any other way."

The obvious goal of SVT was to create a Mustang Cobra that re-cast the very image of the team's iconic flagship. But the overwhelming success of the Terminator project had greater ramifications for Ford Motor Company as an entity.

"You need a car to establish the credentials and create the aspirations for everybody," explains John Coletti. "It becomes the halo car for the whole fleet. And that's what the Cobra does."

"The Cobra is that pinnacle car that kids have on posters on their walls, and they dream of having it," elaborates Alan Hall. "Maybe as they grow up they've got an old 5.0-liter that they're working on, and maybe when they get their first job they can't quite afford a Cobra but they get a Mustang GT – but they're still hoping. It's that aspirational product. That's what we want them to keep yearning for."

The crowds that gathered around the Terminator at each auto show appearance and the waiting lists for orders offered proof that aspiration was just one of the emotions engendered by the new Cobra.

The passion of John Coletti and Ford's Special Vehicle Team had been fully channeled into an extraordinary production Mustang that set standards for power and handling that leapt far beyond anything that had ever emerged from Dearborn Assembly Plant. There's no denying that the Ford Mustang's four-decade existence is illuminated by celebrated models including the Boss 302, the Mach 1 Cobra Jet, and the Boss 429 – yet the 2003 SVT Mustang Cobra is more powerful than all of them.

Still, the question must be asked: in years to come, will the name "Terminator" inspire the same reverence as the legends of the first muscle car era?

"Oh, absolutely!" believes Tom Scarpello. "If you think back to what made those cars what they are, they brought a whole new performance proposition to the market. They really kind of turned things on their ear, in terms of how people thought about a particular vehicle, and I think the 2003 Cobra has done the same thing. It's such a huge step forward.

"I definitely think that twenty or thirty years from now, if you go to a car show you're going to see a lot of pristine, restored 2003 Cobras. It will be a really popular car, long into the future," he adds.

"I put the Terminator in the same class as the Boss 429," says Romeo Niche Line's Cary Kramp. "There are very close performance numbers between the two cars, though our car will obviously spank the Boss 429 in weight to power ratio and that kind of stuff. I've driven both of those cars. The Terminator, as far as I'm concerned, will be remembered just as well as the Boss 429, and just as well as the Shelbys."

"People think that's the epitome," powertrain engineer Brian Roback says of the Boss 429. "But if you were to jump in a Boss 429 and then jumped in one of these, you'd really see the difference in the era, and how rough and crude they were back then. A lot of power, but you don't have the creature comforts that this does, the handling that this does – and still, the performance!"

"I think without a doubt, this car is always going to be recognized in Mustang history," says Ford dealer Darin Kreiss. "It's got unique features that make it stand alone, and then the simple fact that it's the first production supercharged Mustang ever built – I think it's always going to be recognized very, very well."

"I met a gentleman who's a collector," recounts powertrain engineer Dave Dempster. "He's got a couple of Boss 302s, two 429s, and he's

> **"You need a car to establish the credentials and create the aspirations for everybody. It becomes the halo car for the whole fleet. And that's what the Cobra does."**
>
> **~John Coletti**

got a Shelby as well. But he bought one of these – a red convertible – and he said this is the most fun car. He said, 'This is the most fun car out of all the cars that I have. This is the car that I like driving.'"

"You drive a Mustang GT, or a standard Mustang, or even one of the older Cobras, and it was fun," agrees Romeo Engine's Tom Wilson. "But when you got in this one, and the first time you popped that clutch and stomped on that pedal and you buried your back in that seat – you knew it was something that was going to be remembered."

"Somebody asked me the question, 'John, are these going to be worth something in the future?'" recalls John Coletti. "If I knew that, hell, I wouldn't be working here, if I could predict where the price was going to be. But from a functional standpoint as a total car package, it's certainly a high water mark. It's all there."

"The 2003 Mustang Cobra was a beautiful car, and it was the fastest factory Mustang ever produced," concludes Bill Ford. "History will be the ultimate judge, but I don't see why it shouldn't be ranked among the greatest Mustangs of all time."

Legacy Assured

All vehicles go through development programs that offer stories of obstacles and issues that stood between concept and realization.

But in the case of the Terminator, its tale will stand as one that is unique, with a script not likely to be followed again. Imposing time frames, mercurial leaders, proud auto workers, specialized parts and components, procedures developed on the fly – all characterized the birth of this Cobra.

Despite eighteen months of challenges and tribulations, the result of the Terminator program was strikingly self-evident. And as SVT engineer Scott Tate asked for all of those whose enthusiasm and effort helped shape this singular vehicle, "Who wouldn't want to work on the fastest production Mustang?"

Certainly hundreds of people at Ford Motor Company had reason to be proud of their joint creation: a Mustang that, in years to come, will likely be regarded as a classic American performance car.

"As we grow older I think it's going to be cool to go to the car shows and swap meets and see somebody who's got a Cobra," imagines Brad Lammers. "Just to know you had an impact on that car, and that you touched it and felt it and breathed it for almost two years of your life… There's nothing like that feeling."

Opposite: Ready to make use of their independent rear suspensions, a gaggle of Cobras approach a road course turn during SVT Superfest at Virginia International Raceway. SVT Cobra Mustang Club founder Tony Sorrentino puts on the popular annual event that draws Terminators and other high performance track cars from across the country.
Photo: Marcie Cipriani

CHAPTER 12 AFTERMATH

Opposite: Terminator team members and suppliers proudly signed this large image of the bold new automotive creation. Above: Aside from coupe or convertible and color selections, there were just two choices when it came to 2003-2004 Terminator options. One was to delete the spoiler, the other to upgrade to chrome wheels.

Changes to the Standard

Following the introduction of the Mustang Cobra Terminator in 2002, SVT took limited action to keep the model fresh as the months passed. The Cobra's production run was lengthened to include model year 2004, and while the structure of the car remained identical throughout this period, the color palette was refined. The original selection of seven shades found new choices Dark Shadow Grey and Redfire moving into the lineup halfway through the 2003 run, while Torch Red, Screaming Yellow, and Competition Orange rotated in for 2004.

Indeed, options were few on all the Cobras, with buyers limited to a choice of coupe or convertible, polished or chrome wheels, and one of two interior color packages. It was also possible to select a spoiler-delete option.

Twice during Terminator production, Ford and SVT took steps to freshen interest in the supercharged Mustang Cobras by introducing special trim editions: the 2003 SVT Mustang Cobra 10th Anniversary Edition, and the 2004 SVT Mustang Cobra Mystichrome.

That SVT in 2003 could celebrate an entire decade of existence, not only surviving but thriving, was more than enough reason to add some special

touches to a limited run of Terminators in honor of the occasion. The target number of vehicles to be produced in the run was an easy one to select: 2003 in total.

The 10th Anniversary run crossed the spectrum of the Mustang Cobra platform, with both coupes and convertibles bearing special badging complementing three color choices: Black, Silver Metallic, or a vibrant Torch Red. All of the 10th Anniversary cars rolled on a new design wheel, boasted red brake calipers, had red leather seating inserts, and included interiors with a special leather trim for the steering wheel, shift boot, and parking brake handle.

There was just one color choice available for the 2004 Mustang Cobra Mystichrome production – but what color you saw depended on where you were standing.

The Mystichrome paint applied on the 1,010 coupes and convertibles selected for this production run was specially conjured up by DuPont. Using a unique pigment that reflects white light into visible colors, the company mixed this potent brew with traditional black and green. The result was a batch of Terminators with body colors that appeared to shift from green to purple to blue to black. Matching steering wheel treatment, interior seat inserts, and chrome wheels topped off a package that understandably generated excitement – although as years passed the difficulty of obtaining and high cost of purchasing the Mystichrome paint from current-formula-owner BASF turned out to be an area of real concern for owners of these unique Mustang Cobras.

2003 10th Anniversary SVT Cobra. Production totalled 2,003 units in red, silver and black.

Photos: Ford Motor Company, Marcie Cipriani

2004 SVT Cobra in color-shifting
Mystichrome paint. A total of 1,010
were produced. Detailed production
numbers can be found in the appendix.
Photos: Ford Motor Company, Marcie Cipriani

Closing the Books

Despite the presence of the two special trim editions, it was inevitable: time marched on. And no matter how fast the vehicles built by SVT went, they couldn't outrun the changes that came with the passing of the seasons.

Still, the supercharged Mustang Cobra developed from late 2000 through early 2002 had unprecedented and lengthy reign over the streets, drag strips, road courses, and highways where the Mustang legend continues to be written more than a decade later. This Cobra ably represented Ford's Special Vehicle Team and the company's high performance profile during a years-long gap between the Terminator's introduction in 2002 and the arrival of the next performance Mustang – code-named "Condor" – in the form of the 2007 Shelby GT500. It was a span imposed by the mainstream Mustang's migration to the S197 hybrid platform for the model year 2005.

Of course, in the realm of performance cars, it's predictable that a more powerful iteration will eventually make its own proud debut, to the acclaim of the automotive media and the open checkbooks of the enthusiasts. That was proven upon the revelation of the newer GT500, with its official rating of 500 horsepower. And while cynics argued that the Shelby needed that extra power to haul its bulk around – the car

weighed over 250 pounds, or seven percent, more than the Terminator – it too was an impressive vehicle, even with a live rear axle suspension in place of the independent designs that were a valuable performance hallmark of the predecessor Mustang Cobras.

Still, as *Car and Driver* noted in a review of that new Shelby, "our GT500 test coupe wasn't any quicker than the (2003) SVT Mustang Cobra." Clearly, there was no arguing that the 2003 Cobra had set new standards and written its own distinctive chapter in the history of the Ford Mustang.

As production of the Terminator came to an end, the Romeo Engine Plant Niche Line scaled back. The number of teams was reduced as the builders focused their talents on crafting a relative handful of supercharged Ford GT engines. This powerplant – the heart of Ford's hotly-anticipated supercar – easily made 550 horsepower.

Considering the Ford GT and the new Cobra were designed side-by-side by Camilo Pardo, it's appropriate that the GT program became a home away from home for some of the SVT personnel who migrated elsewhere within Ford upon completion of the Terminator development effort. Among those who contributed to bringing the GT to market in 2004 were Cobra program manager Tom Bochenek and team manager Primo Goffi.

Above: Artist's rendering of the 'Condor' project – SVT's codename for its 2006 SVT Mustang Cobra program.
Right: The now-retired Ellen Collins was Coletti's program manager for 'Condor,' the S-197 SVT Cobra which became the Shelby GT500.
Photos courtesy John Clor

The Terminator benefits from an obvious aerodynamic advantage compared to the flat snout of its newer GT500 cousin. The latter boasts more horsepower, but that's a necessity due to its increased weight.

Photos: Frank Moriarty, Ford Motor Company

Two muscular stances: the modern classicism of Camilo Pardo's Terminator design, and the heavily retro-flavored GT500.

Photos: Frank Moriarty, Ford Motor Company

Mark Dipko, who led efforts to hone the Terminator vehicle dynamics, left SVT and Ford to become a marketing manager at Yamaha Motor Corporation – and never had the opportunity to drive the finished tuning of his work.

"To tell you the truth, I have never driven the car after leaving, so I am not sure what the result was," he says. "It was kind of bittersweet for me since I wasn't there during the press launches and Job One like I was for the Cobra R."

But many of the engineers who contributed to the Terminator remained under the SVT banner, laboring to bring the next generation of the team's developments to fruition – although new security around SVT's offices reduced the likelihood of trespassing photographers catching glimpses of works in progress.

The author and John Coletti wrap up a spirited session of bench racing and Terminator talk in the office of SVT's leader in 2004.
Photo: Marcie Cipriani

Ending an Era

On a March day in 2004 I met with John Coletti to talk about the Terminator. His schedule looked to be typically hectic; he had "maybe thirty minutes." After all, SVT was still riding the crest of a wave of success. The Terminator had been heaped with praise, claiming the cover of most automotive magazines. And the SVT-engineered Ford GT was hailed as a true American supercar, costly for a domestic vehicle yet one that justifiably called to mind comparisons to the legendary GT40 that had inspired it.

Simply put, as the head of the organization that had created these masterpieces, Coletti was a busy man. But ensconced in his corner office on a sunny afternoon, talking about SVT and the performance cars his team developed, time began sailing by.

"The mindset here, I have to tell you – how you really felt…" Coletti began. Then he laughed. "If you don't capture it real time, it's hard to go back and wonder, 'How did I really feel on that day when we were on our eighth engine explosion?'"

But Coletti's modesty over his ability to recall the details of each setback paled compared to his pride in the work of his team – even if his management style had origins in the General George Patton School of Getting Things Done.

"Look at our track record, every program that we've got on the street has been the same dynamic," he admitted. "'John, it's too hard, it's too this' – whine, whine, and whine. And then they deliver. That's the dynamic. But we've worked together for so long, you just…" Coletti paused, then leaned forward. "See, I know what their mentality is," he confided. "You've just got to push them a little bit. And then, they're all happy about what they do when they do it." Like when Tom Chapman found out you'd added over a hundred pounds to his chassis dynamics by going with a supercharger on the Terminator, I ventured?

"Yeah, well… I told him, 'Tom, go make it work' – and he did. He whines, too. 'Oh, do you know what you guys just did to me? You gave me 160 pounds more weight up front!' OK, so get to work – what are you bitching for? And he pulled it off – that car is very nice. The guys did a nice job, but you've got to put up with that whining part of it. Because they all want you to know how much work it is, so that you really fully appreciate the result, right?" he asked with a conspiratorial smile.

The impression I got from everyone at SVT was that working for John Coletti could be intense, demanding, and that, if ever a cliché was proven true, when Coletti said "Jump!" the proper response was, "How high?" And not a single person ever hinted at a negative thought about "the man in the corner office." Instead, every mention of Coletti's name came with a distinct air of fierce loyalty.

"You have to remember who our leader is," said one SVT engineer. "It's John Coletti – the guy who saved the '94 Mustang against everybody's wishes in this company. He kept that car alive and he pissed off everybody below the top of the house doing it. But that's why John Coletti is the man that he is."

"We had the program's horsepower right where it was planned to be," one engineer told me of the soon-to-be-scrapped 2002 Cobra. "But as is John's normal way, it's not quite enough... But we're used to the pressure. He could come up with anything, and we'll go for it. I think it's great. Maybe to a fault, we all think like racers."

"If you know or have read anything about John Coletti," said another, "he's pretty passionate about the vehicles that we do, and hence he gets emotional about things. He says what's on his mind, he's frank and to the point."

Coletti himself chalked it all up to the thing he was most proud of – SVT's vehicles.

"Well, there is the halo effect that you get," he noted. "When you put these kinds of products out there, it says a lot about your product prowess – you can do this stuff, some good stuff. And that's not appropriate for the mass market – you don't need to have supercharged 4.6 engines in every car out there, right? But the fact that you can put it on the market..."

That was the reward, that these great machines were made available to an audience that appreciated them and loved driving them.

"I'll do all this for you," Coletti said of the Terminator. "I'll give you a warranty, make sure it drives nice, sounds nice, and does everything for you – and included in our price is the bigger transmission, bigger clutch, aluminum flywheel. We put all that stuff together – and I told the guys,

John Coletti proudly looks over just a tiny portion of the impressive high performance hardware that emerged from SVT's operations.
Photo: Ford Motor Company

'We're probably giving the enthusiast close to $10,000 worth of stuff, and he's got a warranty to boot!'"

You could tell it pleased him to no end.

"That's why it's what I drive," he said, picking up momentum and talking about the Terminator he personally had purchased. "The first year, in 1999 I had a Lightning, and I've had Cobras since. It's just... This car, especially. When you pull out – see, I do cross-town driving, and if you didn't have that... Sometimes when you break loose from the traffic? In this car, you can really break loose! Ha! You can air it out, and it just seems to flush away all of that anxiety that builds up. It's therapeutic."

The therapy carried over to Coletti's visits to race tracks and drag strips, to see firsthand how SVT products were being received.

"I went to one event here, and nine Cobras showed up. The slowest one was 11.20 – and these are cars that people are driving in!" he marveled. "They drive it in to the track, they beat the shit out of it – 'Yeah, I'm gonna drive it home, because it will hold together.' When's the last time you saw an 11-second car that's streetable? I saw three guys run 10.9s – I couldn't believe it!"

Coletti's great cheer over this potential for power – and the realization of that power by SVT's performance-loving consumers – symbolically pointed directly at the roots of the fundamental difference of opinion that so often lies between car man and car management.

"We're happy about it, but my point is, what we did is nothing. What the guys on the outside are doing with this... Management's sitting there saying, do we want to encourage this kind of stuff? Well, hell yes, you want to encourage that kind of stuff! It's all about image. That snake, that '03 car, when you see that snake, nobody's going to toy with you."

John Coletti was clearly thrilled that he was able to give $10,000 worth of performance value to other car guys for far less than it cost to develop. Yet certain elements of Ford's management hierarchy apparently were not so enamored over the return in investment.

"Everybody recognizes that we do a good job and get the product out there and we're doing the right thing, but they also have that 'not invented here' syndrome," noted one SVT engineer of "mainstream" Ford. "They complain, 'We're not getting credit for it,' and so if they can take a stab at us, they'll take a stab at us."

"Within North American Product Development, of mainstream Ford, we're kind of the good ol' boys," said another. "We're seen as the kind of the people who don't have real careers and want to play in the sandbox for the rest of their lives."

But during 2004, the sandbox suddenly began to get boundaries.

Surprisingly, and despite the acclaim that SVT's first decade of existence brought to Ford Motor Company, late in that year gossip began swirling that the organization was doomed. The tales began when SVT announced it was canceling the next edition of the Lightning pickup program. As the rumors picked up momentum, speculation increased that SVT would soon be no more, a victim of internal Ford power struggles and corporate maneuvering.

An indication that an ill wind just might be blowing came when Tom Scarpello, who deftly aligned SVT's marketing efforts with John Coletti's engineering focus, left the team, taking a marketing vice president position with Jaguar North America on November 15.

Then things began happening quickly. Just four days later, Chris Theodore, Ford's vice president overseeing Advanced Product Creation, left the company. Theodore was an SVT advocate, and team members confided that without his enthusiastic support, Coletti was certain to face uphill battles with regard to program approvals.

The picture changed further when Ford announced that, effective December 1, 2004, Hau Thai-Tang would assume the responsibilities of Theodore's product creation post as well as directing the operations of the Special Vehicle Team. Prior to this appointment, Thai-Tang was Chief Nameplate Engineer for the retro-themed 2005 Ford Mustang, and he'd led the development and launch of the 2001 Mustang GT, Mustang Cobra, and Bullitt Mustang GT models. John Coletti was to continue as director of the Special Vehicle Team, reporting to Thai-Tang.

Hau Thai-Tang
Photo: Ford Motor Company

"The appointment of Hau to this role further cements the importance of SVT to Ford," claimed Phil Martens, Ford Product Creation group vice president and Thai-Tang's boss. Yet whispers in the industry carried the message that Martens was anything but a fan of SVT and it's "go fast at all costs" mantra, let alone Coletti's management style.

In an interview shortly after his appointment, Thai-Tang insisted that SVT would be returning to its roots, yet would strive to have "broader appeal" in its offerings. SVT's fans could be forgiven for feeling a touch of uncertainty about the implications of such a forecast. Many felt the idea of SVT being incorporated into the Ford mainstream was sheer blasphemy.

One thing was certain however – never again would a Mustang Cobra emerge newly-built from the historic Dearborn Assembly Plant. On May 10, 2004, a red convertible Mustang became the final pony car to roll off the assembly line as Ford closed the plant after more than eighty years of production, half of them dedicated to the Mustang.

Six weeks earlier, on March 31, 2004, the last Cobra was built, also a red convertible. Appropriately, this vehicle ended up in the possession of Larry Plopan, a DAP employee who had worked in the plant for nearly thirty-five years. After ordering his Cobra through a local SVT dealer as production neared its end, he put in a request that his order be the last one filled. He was surprised when his wish was granted.

"This car got a lot of attention, and I got to watch it get built," Plopan told *Mustang Times*. "Being the last Cobra, many of the workers on the line assumed this car was being built for some high-ranking executive. When I told them it was for me, some of the assembly workers on the line asked if they could sign it. Since it was my car, I said, 'Sure, why not?' So on the underside of my car on the floor pan, while the car was being built, a lot of people signed my car…

> **"I lived through the muscle car era – but this is the golden age of performance."**
>
> **~John Coletti**

"The closing of the plant is like the death of an empire," Plopan said. "When we built the Mustang, it really was something special. We were the only plant building the Mustang so we got a lot of special attention that no other plant got."

While many of the DAP workers were assured of employment building F-150 pickups at a new facility, Tommy Demeester, who had acted on behalf of the plant workers in discussions with SVT about the Cobra, retired after thirty-two years with Ford. And Dave Diegel, lured from retirement after a career with GM and hired by SVT to interface with the plant, announced his second retirement from the auto industry.

The attitude of DAP's workers had been characterized by their excitement about building Cobra variations. So understandably, some SVT engineers were uneasy about the closure of DAP and the inception of a partnership with the new AutoAlliance International plant. This facility, in Flat Rock, MI, became the home of Mustang assembly beginning with the 2005 model. At AAI, 2005 Mustang production was shared with Mazda production in a joint venture with Ford that yielded a manufacturing stew of six- and eight-cylinder rear wheel drive cars as well as four- and six-cylinder front wheel drive vehicles.

"We're already seeing, moving the new product into a new assembly plant that just doesn't have a history with Mustang, it's 'OK, it's just another job,'" one SVT engineer told me at the time. "And that's just more complexity."

"We've got a long road ahead of us with the next program," agreed another, "because at AAI you're just another car."

But those concerns paled in comparison to the impact of an announcement made by Ford Motor Company on December 12, 2004: John Coletti, after thirty-two years with Ford, was retiring. Coming in the wake of the recent organizational changes for SVT, most weren't surprised by Coletti's sudden "personal decision." He politely averred that he had been pondering retirement since March.

Meanwhile, Hau Thai-Tang began his command from an office located not within SVT's confines, but near that of Phil Martens in Ford's Product Development Center.

Soon after, more indications became apparent that things were different under SVT's new regime. Tellingly, the Condor program, begun under Coletti, would not be marketed as an SVT Mustang Cobra – making the Terminator the eighth and final iteration of a high performance model that had become legendary. Instead, SVT badging was downplayed when the Shelby Cobra GT500 concept was revealed in March, 2005. In fact, the production model of the new Mustang variation dropped the word "Cobra" entirely from its name in favor of playing up Carroll Shelby's return to Ford – although there were opinions voiced that Shelby's actual involvement had consisted of little more than offering feedback from rides in prototypes.

SVT's dealership network was not thrilled with the Shelby GT500 program for another reason. Instead of selling the car as an SVT vehicle exclusively through authorized SVT dealers – dealers who paid a not-inconsequential fee for elite performance status – the Shelby was made available to all Ford dealers.

"They just decided to hang the loyal SVT dealers out and give the car to everyone," one long-time SVT dealer told me. "We're the people who have paid for this program since the inception with our SVT franchise fees, all the while being told in the lean years that if we get out of the program we won't be allowed back in for the strong years. Can you tell I'm very angry with their decision?"

More bad news arrived in January 2006 when Ford announced a sweeping cost-cutting program dubbed the "Way Forward" plan. Like all areas operating within the auto manufacturer, SVT was targeted for severe cutbacks.

Clearly, the world of the Special Vehicle Team had changed radically on nearly every level. Bob Lewis, who oversaw SVT's relationship with its dealers and also chaired the Dealer Advisory Board, had once explained to me that "we are to some extent very similar to a small car company." But now SVT – in its prime overseeing its own engineering, marketing, sales, and public relations operations with the goal of selling product through its own certified dealer network – had been fully assimilated back into the monolithic Ford corporate structure.

Regardless of the events that forced Coletti's departure from the team he had helped guide to world-class stature, there is no disputing the impact he had at Ford and upon his co-workers.

While working on this book project, I spoke with Tom Scarpello on the phone one afternoon about the Cobra program. Minutes later the phone rang again. It was Scarpello, wanting to further stress John Coletti's importance to SVT and the realization of the Terminator.

"There aren't many people in a company that would have accepted that level of challenge," Scarpello emphasized. "The downside risk was tremendous, and the upside wasn't that great, so I really have to give him credit for stepping up and saying, 'Hey, we're going to give this our best shot and we're going to go for it.' Because in what's normally a very risk-averse culture, that was an uncharacteristic decision. I think, though, it's very indicative of our organization and why we're able to do the kinds of things that we do. So I just wanted to make sure that I mentioned that, because it's pretty important.

"He was putting his own reputation on the line because he was the guy that ultimately was going to take responsibility for it if it didn't get done," he continued. "I can say that between he and I, we share responsibility for the business, and that's a true statement, but when it actually comes down to engineering the vehicle and meeting the deliverable, it's his name on the performance review for that. So he signed up to it, and I have to give him credit for that, because if he hadn't done it, I don't know of anybody else that would have stepped up to that challenge. John really is the guy that deserves credit for the 2003 Cobra being the way that it is."

As if to offer full realization of both John Coletti's vision and the Terminator's potential, shortly before the announcement of Coletti's retirement came news that SVT and the Ford Racing Performance Parts group had teamed up on a special project. The idea: take many of the FRPP catalog parts applicable to the Terminator, bolt them on, and see what happens.

The result was an amazing 690-horsepower monster, born from simple modifications costing less than $14,000. In fact, the complete cost of the 2004 Cobra itself and the parts enhancing its already formidable performance numbers was just $47,033.75. And that vehicle's imposing power level was a goal that some observers believed could never be obtained by the new GT500, as its engine lacked the Manley rods and "bulletproof" foundation that would successfully host such aggressive modification.

Ford Racing Performance Parts' imposing 690-horsepower Terminator – the answer to the ultimate SVT Mustang Cobra "what if?" question.
Photos: Ford Motor Company

The conclusion was simple: the Terminator had been a relative bargain, boasting an ability to reliably crank out staggering horsepower. And no doubt that had made John Coletti a happy man.

It was this passion for performance that drove Coletti and his fellow visionaries, at Ford Motor Company and elsewhere in the auto industry, to begin the new millennium by ushering in a fresh era of automotive high performance after decades of meager horsepower and sluggish handling. Once again, muscular cars were rumbling down the streets of America, but now they were emboldened with new benchmarks of sophistication in suspension and powertrain development.

As John Coletti himself told me after our wide-ranging discussion of the Terminator and Ford GT programs, "I lived through the muscle car era – but this is the golden age of performance."

EPILOGUE The Legacy Lives On

Birds of a Feather

Petunia and Terminator. Development code names for an automotive odd couple.

One was destined to become a costly supercar based on a legendary story that had played out four decades before. The other was faster and more powerful than its forerunners, but still intended to be within the financial reach of the average person on the streets.

Yet somehow, they were perfect together. And designer Camilo Pardo could see this synchronicity as he worked on both cars side-by-side, their personalities emerging as he thoughtfully revealed each car's character in a clandestine satellite design studio.

The Ford GT – aka Petunia – presented Pardo with the challenge of modernizing an iconic predecessor, the Ford GT40. But since no iteration of that car had been built since the 1960s, something of a clean slate was at hand, offering Pardo a significant measure of creative freedom.

Opposite: Model A, meet Model T – Terminator, that is. Amazingly, Rich Wenzke's beautiful 1931 Ford and this 2003 SVT Mustang Cobra were built in the very same assembly plant – more than seven decades apart.
Photo: Frank Moriarty

The SVT Mustang Cobra? Well, the Terminator presented a more thorny issue. Everyone knew that, within months, the Ford Mustang would move to a new generation with the S-197 platform. How to turn heads with a tired body style that was nearing its tenth birthday?

The answer was to cross the DNA of the bold new GT with the firmly-established and familiar Mustang, the performance heritage that flavored the GT program adding spice to the Terminator.

A hallmark of the GT was its prominent and dramatic front scoops, beginning on the top surface of the car at the front wheels and fading back toward the windshield. Pardo took this design cue and, though the scoops were smaller in dimension, boldly applied this concept to the Terminator's hood. In the wake of the scoops appeared two long channels that gracefully arced to the windshield base.

Larger round fog lamps rode low on both cars, gliding just over the pavement and offering illumination from the corners of their sleek front fascia. The large scooped air cavity on the Terminator's fascia echoed the opening that graced a similar location on the GT.

The uninterrupted flow of the GT's side surfaces down toward the ground was implemented by Pardo on the Terminator as well. The designer smoothed out the side skirt areas below the doors, yielding a cleaner shape than that found on the other production Mustangs of the era.

All of the imagery, imagination, and intangibles applied to this car by Camilo Pardo gave this generation of the SVT Mustang Cobra an imposing and striking bearing. Its stance telepathically implanted images of power and handling in the mind of anyone who came across the Terminator.

And then there was the fact that John Coletti and his team devised components and systems underneath the rejuvenated body that more than fulfilled the promise of Pardo's design.

Put it all together and it was truly a complete performance package, every aspect of the Mustang Cobra elevated to heady new levels.

Photo: Frank Moriarty

Taking a Place in History

But how can we judge the long-term significance of the 2003-2004 Ford SVT Mustang Cobra?

An honest answer to that question requires the passage of time and the emergence of perspective. Now, more than a full decade after the Terminator emerged from skunkworks secrecy, its place in the history books is beginning to be written.

In 2013 John Clor, a respected Ford authority, journalist, and author of the acclaimed comprehensive history *The Mustang Dynasty*, took on the challenge of ranking SVT's Mustang Cobra creations for a feature in *Mustang Monthly* magazine. Number one? The Terminator.

"The Terminator Cobra will go down in history as SVT's benchmark performance Mustang," Clor judged. "Thanks to its Eaton supercharged DOHC 4.6-liter with forged internals, its 390hp rating has often been doubled by racers."

That is an impressive fact, but is horsepower the bottom line?

Manufacturers now commonly implant engines rated at 400, 500, 600, and even 700 horsepower into their automotive hosts. But are they truly engineering a top-to-bottom, end-to-end performance entity, or just throwing horsepower at heavy, bloated foundations resulting in ill-handling vehicles bearing big numbers?

The Terminator was the pinnacle achievement of SVT's nearly organic skill, the team expert at realizing maximum performance potential finely tuned into mechanical harmony.

And that song was a reliable one. *Motor Trend* adopted a Terminator for a multi-month, multi-driver testing session, determined to put Coletti's vision to the real challenge of day-to-day use in a long-term situation.

"This car proved rock solid reliable, in spite of the power it makes and," the magazine admitted, "the thrashing it got when nobody was looking… With every stab of the throttle, seeing the boost gauge flex and hearing the siren-like whine of the supercharger confirmed that this was not simply a muscle car wannabe… There were never any serious mechanical issues – or anything that would have stranded us."

The supercharged reliability from the independent rear suspension Terminator's 4.6-liter engine paved the way for the 5.4-liter supercharged engine that powered the solid-axle Ford Shelby GT500 in 2007 – the successor to the 2003-2004 SVT Mustang Cobra and a car that John Clor ranks several notches below the Terminator's throne at the top of the list.

Interestingly, one of the earliest prototype Terminator engines played a role in an automotive mystery that unfolded in 2015 – and the initial self-published version of the book you are now reading played its part as well.

Signature Required

As detailed in Chapter 11: *Power to the People*, "scout builds" took place in the early phases of production planning for the hand-building of the supercharged Terminator engines along the Niche Line at Romeo Engine Plant. These builds validated processes, procedures, and mechanical aspects planned for the production engines. Playing the role of one of the two-man teams who would soon be responsible for production assembly, SVT powertrain engineer Brian Roback and Brad Lammers, the manufacturing engineer lead for the new SVT Mustang Cobra, built a Terminator engine on the Niche Line months before production began in April 2002.

At the end of the line, though, with the completed pre-production engine before them, they were stymied: the real two-man Niche Line teams got credit for each build under their own names via embossed signature plates featuring the SVT logo. Such plates would be attached to every Terminator engine built on the Niche Line. There was no Roback and Lammers plate. So the two did the next best thing – they took a big blue marker and hand-signed their work the old-fashioned way.

Flash forward almost 15 years, and Lammers receives a message via LinkedIn, from an email address associated with the University of Tennessee.

There were no signature plates ready to be applied to this "scout build" pre-production Cobra engine. Instead, prior to installation in a Terminator prototype revealed to invited guests before the 2002 Chicago Auto Show, the engine was hand-signed – an action that eventually led to a fascinating story about the powerplant's current whereabouts.

"Hey Mr. Lammers, I hope you see this message as I've done some searching and haven't been able to find any answers!" began the message from Matt Haynes. "I have a 2003 Cobra motor with your signature as well as Brian Roback's, with the letters CDK underneath them in thick blue marker. I have read *Iron Fist, Lead Foot* (great read by the way) and found out you hand-built one of the very first motors as a test and signed it…"

Lammers was astonished. A chain of emails began flying through the digital realm, seeking and finding information about the remarkable journey of the engine Brian and Brad had built so long ago.

The two had assumed their engine would simply be used for no more glorious duty than dyno testing; instead, it had been placed in the compartment of a "Colorado Red" prototype convertible, one of the four "1PP" cars that would be the first Terminators officially seen by the public.

After its debut role on February 5, 2002 at the Arlington Heights Ford invite-only reveal, and following floor time duty at the 2002 Chicago Auto Show, the red convertible was either parted out or may have been totaled in an accident. It has a "Branded Title," which means it was sold for salvage or scrap.

No one is sure how, but the Lammers/Roback engine made its way to Arlington, Texas. There, it was bought by a 2003 Ford Mustang

Mach 1 owner from Alabama who decided to upgrade his car's performance potential. Lammers noted in an email to me, "I know there are some companies in Texas that build Ford Engines for service and perhaps they bought and sold it to the original Mach 1 owner."

When Matt Haynes bought the car from the Alabama owner, he was determined to get to the bottom of the strange signatures he found on one of the valve covers. Soon his query landed in Lammers' inbox – and he now has a wild tale to tell about the origins of the engine under the hood of his Mach 1.

That the Terminator is fairly well-documented is unusual in this realm of automotive specialty development. Articles about the Ford GT often note that many early renderings for the GT were destroyed as development moved on; that Camilo Pardo had so many early looks at his Terminator work available to share in this book may have been a happy case of the *Iron Fist, Lead Foot* project getting underway just a handful of months after the car's debut.

In fact, any further delay may have made the creation of this book impossible, because of the turmoil and upheaval that struck Ford's Special Vehicle Team so soon after their greatest triumph.

When the Terminator made its memorable debut at the 2002 Chicago Auto Show, SVT had already amassed a decade's worth of high performance development experience. The vehicles they had applied their magic touch to in the years leading up to the Terminator had focused tremendous attention on the team's activities. But the Terminator ramped that notoriety up sky high.

The automotive world was wondering, "What will they do next?" To be, for all intents and purposes, dismantled, was far from the answer anyone expected. But that's what happened. As *Car and Driver* succinctly put it in a 2006 headline, "Ford Drives Its 13-Year-Old SVT Group Off a Cliff."

First over the edge was John Coletti himself, who in late December 2004 either decided it was time to retire or was shown the emergency exit by those rankled by SVT's independent operations. A key Coletti supporter in Ford's upper management echelon, product executive Chris Theodore, had departed the company weeks earlier.

Did John Coletti upset the smooth path of the corporate apple cart? There's not much doubt about the answer to that question. But did he get results? Well, forget for a moment the thousands and thousands of thrilled Terminator owners all preaching SVT's gospel, and just take a

Is there any doubt that Jay Leno (second from right) is the greatest gearhead party host? Then again, the retirement of John Coletti (far left) deserved nothing less. The influential racer Carroll Shelby (second from left) and legendary driver Dan Gurney (right) join in the fun.
Photo courtesy O. John Coletti

look at all the magazine covers depicting Terminators. They all shined the brightest of automotive spotlights squarely on Ford Motor Company. That is attention and market buzz you cannot buy.

With Coletti gone and no product in 2005, SVT – with its unique and independent engineering, marketing, public relations, and sales entities – was quickly and ruthlessly assimilated into the mainstream Ford product development mothership.

When the fruits of SVT's last labors emerged – in the form of the 2007 GT500 – the letters "SVT" had essentially been replaced by the name "Shelby." It was a final slap in the face to what SVT had once been.

It's ironic that history now reveals the Terminator – a car associated with Mustang firsts like its supercharged engine and Manley connecting rods – may be most significant for its lasts: the last iteration of the Mustang Cobra line, the last days of the Dearborn Assembly Plant, the last glorious skunkworks project of the Special Vehicle Team before its ingestion by mainstream Ford, Coletti's group breaking all the rules binding automotive production but succeeding in spectacular fashion.

Was the Terminator the greatest Mustang ever? Because of its totally unique origins and from a contemporary power, performance, and handling perspective, there are those who would say, "Yes." Surely, that's a matter of opinion.

But there is no disputing that the incredible events around John Coletti and the creation of the 2003-2004 Ford SVT Mustang Cobra – the Terminator – were a convergence of unique circumstances, highly-skilled people, and industrial know-how. And it was all driven by one man who was empowered to make – and unafraid to make – the difficult decisions that others would have shied away from, economic consequences giving way to doing what was right in pursuit of an unwavering vision.

It amounts to an automotive tale the likes of which may never be told again.

2003-2004 FORD MUSTANG SVT COBRA SPECIFICATIONS

APPENDIX
Facts, Figures & Features

PERFORMANCE

HORSEPOWER (SAE net)
Coupe/Convertible   390 @ 6000rpm

TORQUE (SAE net lb-ft)
Coupe/Convertible   390 @ 3500rpm

0-60 time
Coupe   4.5 sec
Convertible   4.6 sec

1/4 MILE (time and speed)
Coupe   12.67 sec, 110.00 mph
Convertible   12.99 sec, 109.85 mph

TOP SPEED
Coupe/Convertible   155 mph (electronically limited)

VEHICLE TYPE
Front-engine, rear-wheel-drive, 2+2-passenger,
2-door coupe or convertible.

CHASSIS/BODY
Type   unit construction
Body material   welded steel stampings

ENGINE
Type   Supercharged and intercooled V-8, iron block and aluminum heads
Manufacturing location   Romeo, Mich.
Configuration   V-8
Intake manifold   Cast aluminum, Tuned equal-length runners
Exhaust manifold   Cast iron
Throttle body   57-mm dual-bore
Mass-air sensor   90mm diameter
Valvetrain   DOHC, 2 valves per cylinder
Valve diameter   Intake: 37 mm
                                 Exhaust: 30 mm
Ignition   Distributorless coil-on-plug
Bore x stroke   3.55 x 3.54 in., 90.2 x 90.0mm
Displacement   281 cu in, 4601cc
Compression ratio   8.5:1

Engine control system   Ford EEC-V with port fuel injection
Supercharger   Eaton M112, Roots type
Maximum boost pressure   8.0 psi
Specific Output   84.8 hp/liter
Redline   6,500 rpm
Fuel capacity   15.7 gal.
Fuel injection   Electronic, sequential
Emission control   3-way catalytic converter, feedback air-fuel-ratio control, EGR
Oil capacity   6.0 quarts

TRANSMISSION
Standard (Type)   TTC T-56 Six-speed manual
Final-drive ratio   3.55:1
GearRatio
I   2.66
II   1.78
III   1.30
IV   1.00
V   0.80
VI   0.63

CLUTCH   11.0 in. single plate

DRIVESHAFT   Aluminum, with hardened yoke, 1350 U-Joints

REAR AXLE   8.8 in. ring gear with 3.55:1 limited slip differential, aluminum case

EXHAUST SYSTEM
Dual, stainless steel, 2.25 in. diameter,
3.0 in. polished exhaust tips

TIRES AND WHEELS
Wheel size   17 x 9 in
Wheel type   five spoke cast aluminum alloy, machined surface, exposed lugs
Tires   Goodyear Eagle F1 GS, P275/40ZR-17 98W

SUSPENSION

Front: Modified Macpherson strut system with gas-charged Bilstein™ mono-tube dampers and separate 600 lb/in coil springs (convertible - 500 lb/in), 29mm tubular stabilizer bar

Rear: Multi-link independent system, cast iron upper control arms, aluminum lower control arms, fixed toe-control tie rods, aluminum spindles, gas-charged Bilstein™ monotube dampers, 600 lb/in coil springs (convertible - 470 lb/in), 26mm tubular stabilizer bar

STEERING

Type	rack-and-pinion, power-assisted
Turns lock-to-lock	2.5
Turning circle curb-to-curb	37.9 ft

BRAKES

Front	13.0 vented Brembo™ disc, PBR™ twin-piston caliper
Rear	11.7 vented disc, single-piston caliper
ABS	four-channel, four-sensor system

DIMENSIONS AND CAPACITIES

EXTERIOR

Wheelbase	101.3 in.
Overall length	183.5 in.
Overall width	73.1 in.
Overall height	52.5 in.
Track width, front/rear	60.3 in. / 60.3 in.

INTERIOR

Seating capacity	4
Passenger volume front	49 cu. ft.
Passenger volume rear	32 cu. ft.
Cargo volume	11 cu. ft.
Front seats	bucket
Seat adjustments	fore and aft, seatback angle, height, lumbar, and lateral support

BASE CURB WEIGHT

Curb weight	3,665 lbs. coupe
	3,780 lbs. convertible
Weight distribution (f/r)	56.6/43.4%

SAFETY

Restraint systems, front	manual 3-point belts, driver and passenger airbags, rear - manual 3-point belts

EXTERIOR/INTERIOR COLORS

Exterior colors	Oxford White, Ebony, Torch Red, Red Fire, Silver Metallic 2003 only: Sonic Blue, Zinc Yellow, Satin Silver Metallic, Mineral Grey Metallic, Dark Shadow Grey 2004 only: Screaming Yellow, Competition Orange, Mystichrome
Interior color	Dark Charcoal with seat inserts in: Medium Parchment, Medium Graphite, Dark Charcoal, Red Leather (10th Anniv 2003 edition), Mystichrome (2004 Mystichrome edition)

STANDARD EQUIPMENT

Major standard accessories: power steering,windows, seats, and locks; A/C; cruise control; tilting steering wheel; rear defroster

Sound system: Ford/Mach AM/FM-stereo radio / CD changer, 6 speakers

OPTIONAL EQUIPMENT

Rear spoiler delete
Chrome wheels

Cobra unique standard features

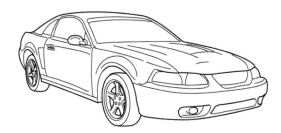

- 4.6L DOHC 32V Supercharged V–8 Engine with Intercooler — 390 horsepower, 390 lb-ft torque
- T56 6–speed transmission
- Aluminum flywheel
- Engine oil cooler
- Power steering cooler
- Anti-lock Brake System with Traction Control℠
- Independent rear suspension with limited-slip differential
- SVT-tuned suspension and brakes
- 17"x 9"cast-aluminum wheels
- P275/40ZR17 BSW Performance Tires
- Specially tuned stainless steel exhaust system
- Decklid spoiler, hood, rocker moldings, front and rear fascia
- Round fog lamps
- Color keyed fold-away mirrors
- Unique cloth top (convertible only)
- Interval wipers with aerodynamic wiper/blade
- Electroluminescent cluster with mechanical boost gauge
- Sport seats with adjustable-driver bolsters and leather and preferred suede seating surfaces
- Sport pedals with aluminum covers
- Leather-wrapped sport steering wheel

2003-2004 SVT Cobra VIN Decoder
(VEHICLE IDENTIFICATION NUMBER)

1FA FP49Y43F 100001

1FA - Ford Motor Company
F - Restraint system (F-Driver/Pass Airbag)
P49 - Body style (48-2-door Coupe, 49-2-door Conv)
Y - Engine code
4 - Check digit
3 - Year (3-2003, 4-2004)
F - Plant (Dearborn)
100001 - Consecutive unit number

Engine Code

Y - 4.6 liter DOHC, S/C EFI, V-8, 390hp

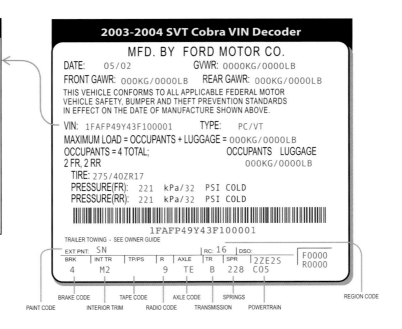

2003-2004 SVT Cobra VIN Decoder

MFD. BY FORD MOTOR CO.

DATE: 05/02   GVWR: 0000KG/0000LB
FRONT GAWR: 000KG/0000LB   REAR GAWR: 000KG/0000LB
THIS VEHICLE CONFORMS TO ALL APPLICABLE FEDERAL MOTOR VEHICLE SAFETY, BUMPER AND THEFT PREVENTION STANDARDS IN EFFECT ON THE DATE OF MANUFACTURE SHOWN ABOVE.

VIN: 1FAFP49Y43F100001   TYPE: PC/VT
MAXIMUM LOAD = OCCUPANTS + LUGGAGE = 000KG/0000LB
OCCUPANTS = 4 TOTAL;   OCCUPANTS   LUGGAGE
2 FR, 2 RR   000KG/0000LB
TIRE: 275/40ZR17
PRESSURE(FR): 221 kPa/32 PSI COLD
PRESSURE(RR): 221 kPa/32 PSI COLD

1FAFP49Y43F100001

TRAILER TOWING - SEE OWNER GUIDE

EXT PNT: SN   RC: 16   DSO: F0000 R0000
BRK | INT TR | TP/PS | R | AXLE | TR | SPR | 2ZE2S
4 | M2 | | 9 | TE | B | 228 | C05

BRAKE CODE   TAPE CODE   AXLE CODE   SPRINGS   REGION CODE
PAINT CODE   INTERIOR TRIM   RADIO CODE   TRANSMISSION   POWERTRAIN

Exterior Paint Codes:
UA - Black Clearcoat
D3 - Torch Red Clearcoat
Z1 - Oxford White Clearcoat
YN - Silver Clearcoat Metallic
TK - Mineral Grey Metallic
G2 - Redfire Clearcoat Metallic
SN - Sonic Blue
B7 - Zinc Yellow
TL - Satin Silver Metallic
CX - Dark Shadow Grey
G6 - Mystichrome
D6 - Screaming Yellow
CY - Competition Orange

2003 - COUPES

Int. Trim / Body Color ▶ ▼	Black (UA)	Torch Red (D3)	Oxford White (Z1)	Silver Metallic (YN)	Mineral Gray Metallic (TK)	Red Fire (G2)	Sonic Blue (SN)	Zinc Yellow (B7)	Satin Silver Metallic (TL)	Dark Shadow Grey (CX)	Total
M2 Med. Graphite	1,618	214	451	735	302	758	1,029	490	242	851	6,690
MH Med. Parchment	252	59	170	0	0	197	23	0	0	0	701
MR Red Leather	381	365	0	257	0	0	0	0	0	0	1,003
Total Coupes	**2,251**	**638**	**621**	**992**	**302**	**955**	**1,052**	**490**	**242**	**851**	**8,394**

2003 – CONVERTIBLES

	Black	Torch Red	Oxford White	Silver Metallic	Mineral Gray	Red Fire	Sonic Blue	Zinc Yellow	Satin Silver	Dark Shadow	Total
M2 Graphite /Black Rf.	1,095	150	171	311	154	403	340	319	81	446	3,470
M2 Graphite /Parch Rf.	0	7	0	0	0	11	0	0	0	0	18
MH Parch./Black Roof	68	0	7	0	0	0	2	0	0	0	77
MH Parch./Parch. Roof	122	56	130	0	0	196	13	0	0	0	517
MR Red/Black Roof	394	369	0	237	0	0	0	0	0	0	1,000
Total Convertibles	**1,679**	**582**	**308**	**548**	**154**	**610**	**355**	**319**	**81**	**446**	**5,082**

Total 2003 Production 13,476

2004 - COUPES

Interior Trim / Body Color ▶ ▼	Black (UA)	Torch Red (D3)	Oxford White (Z1)	Silver Metallic (YN)	Red Fire (G2)	Mysti-chrome (G6)	Screaming Yellow (D6)	Competition Orange (CY)	Total
M2 Medium Graphite	210	164	120	227	191	0	0	0	912
MW Dark Charcoal	610	313	196	324	318	0	299	281	2,341
MD Mystichrome	0	0	0	0	0	515	0	0	515
Total Coupes	**820**	**477**	**316**	**551**	**509**	**515**	**299**	**281**	**3,768**

2004 – CONVERTIBLES

	Black	Torch Red	Oxford White	Silver Metallic	Red Fire	Mystichrome	Screaming Yellow	Competition Orange	Total
M2 Graphite/Black Roof	84	35	34	94	50	0	0	0	297
MW Charcoal/Black Roof	308	132	94	172	159	0	167	72	1,104
MD Mystichrome./Black Roof	0	0	0	0	0	495	0	0	495
Total Convertibles	**392**	**167**	**128**	**266**	**209**	**495**	**167**	**72**	**1,896**

Total 2004 Production 5,664

PRODUCTION TIMELINE

May 8, 2002: 2003 Model Year production began ▷ **March 31, 2004:** 2004 Model Year production ended

Total produced: 19,140

PRE-PRODUCTION UNITS

#	VIN	Build Date	Style	Color	Interior Trim	Wheels	Emissions	Comments
1	1FAFP48Y12F124873	1/30/02	CPE	UA: Ebony	M2: Graphite	Chrome	49 State	Plant vehicle
2	1FAFP48Y02F120569	1/31/02	CPE	Z1: Oxford White	M2: Graphite	Machined	49 State	Durability car
3	1FAFP48Y72F120570	1/28/02	CPE	B7: Zinc Yellow	M2: Graphite	Machined	49 State	Management car
4	1FAFP49Y02F120571	2/1/02	CVT	D3: Colorado Red	M2: Graphite	Machined	49 State	Auto show car
5	1FAFP48Y32F137916	1/25/02	CPE	D3: Colorado Red	MH: Parchment	Machined	Canada	8-hr durability car

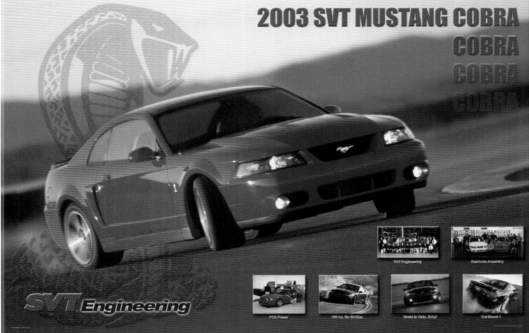

A car as bold as the Terminator was a natural for poster presentation, with three of these images being available at Ford dealers at different points of the model's retail lifespan. The lower left poster was an internal Ford poster – and a valued acquisition for SVT fans.

Photos: Joe Goffin, Marcie Cipriani

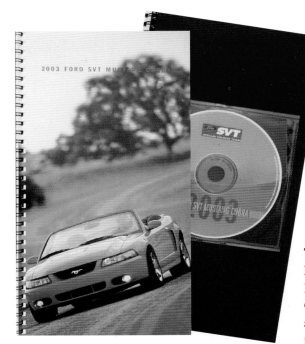

The 2003 Media Press Kit including a CD of images and technical information.
Photo: Joe Goffin

The acclaimed diecast model builder GMP ran a series of 1:4 scale reproductions of significant Ford powerplants. It was no surprise that the Terminator's supercharged 4.6L engine was a valued part of this series.
Photo: Joe Goffin

Tech cards for 2003 and 2004 Terminator.
Photo: Marcie Cipriani

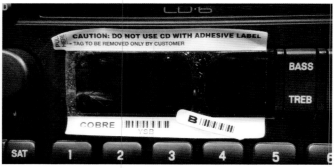

Stickers representing numerous components of vehicle assembly were carefully removed from the SVT Mustang Cobras before the cars were turned over to their new owners – often to the chagrin of collectors who'd prefer to save the documentation of every aspect of their car's creation at Dearborn Assembly Plant.

Photos: Marcie Cipriani

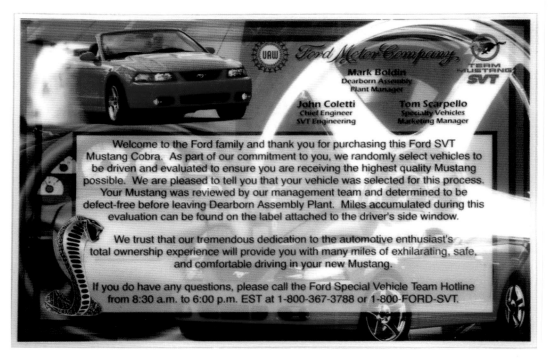

As seen on this notice to owners, certain Terminators were selected for quality check drives. Hopefully these test drives were not as robust as the image seen on the upper left.

Photo: Marcie Cipriani

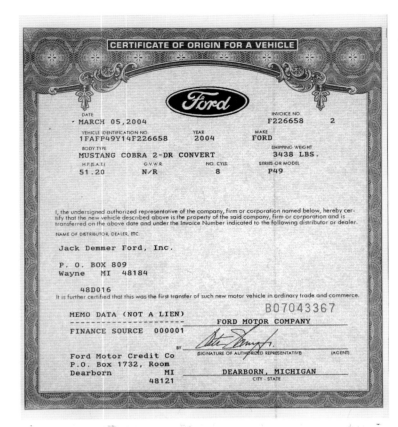

Various official and practical documentation from the assembly process. In the upper left appears a Certificate of Origin (confusingly often referred to by the acronyms MSO or MCO), with the "Broadcast Sheet" above documenting the build. To the left, this engine sheet bears a bright red CB for at-a-glance notification that the engine at hand is Cobra-bound.

Photos: Marcie Cipriani

MAINTENANCE

REFILL CAPACITIES

Fluid	Ford Part Name	Capacity
Brake fluid	Motorcraft High Performance DOT 3 Motor Vehicle Brake Fluid	Fill to line on reservoir
Engine oil (includes filter change)	Motorcraft SAE 5W-20 Super Premium Motor Oil	5.7L (6.0 quarts)
Engine coolant [1]	Motorcraft Premium Engine Coolant (green-colored) or Motorcraft Premium Gold Engine Coolant (yellow-colored)	15.2L (16.1 quarts)
Power steering fluid	Motorcraft MERCON® ATF	Fill to between MIN and MAX lines on reservoir
Rear axle lubricant [2]	Motorcraft SAE 75W-140 High Performance Synthetic Rear Axle Lubricant	1.4L (2.9 pints)
Fuel tank	N/A	59.4L (15.7 gallons)
Intercooler coolant	Motorcraft Premium Engine Coolant (green-colored) or Motorcraft Premium Gold Engine Coolant (yellow-colored)	3.75L (3.96 qts) (see your dealer for service)
Transmission fluid [3]	Refer to the label on your transmission	3.9L (8.2 pints)[4]
Windshield washer fluid	Ultra-Clear Windshield Washer Concentrate	3.8L (4.0 quarts)

[1]Add the coolant type originally equipped in your vehicle.

[2]Rear axle lubricants do not need to be checked or changed unless a leak is suspected, service is required or the axle assembly has been submerged in water. The axle lubricant should be changed any time the rear axle has been submerged in water. Fill 6 mm to 14 mm (1/4 inch to 9/16 inch) below bottom of fill hole. Add 118 ml (4 oz.) of Additive Friction Modifier C8AZ-19B546-A or equivalent meeting Ford specification EST-M2C118–A for complete refill of Traction-Lok axles.

[3]The TTC T56 6–Speed transmission on your SVT Mustang Cobra uses automatic transmission fluid. Ensure the correct automatic transmission fluid is used as indicated in the label on your transmission.

[4]Service refill capacity is determined by filling the transmission to the bottom of the filler hole with the vehicle on a level surface.

MOTORCRAFT PART NUMBERS

Component	4.6L DOHC Supercharged V-8 engine
Air filter element	FA-1632
Fuel filter	FG-800A
Battery	BXT-59
Oil filter	FL-820S
PCV valve	EV-153
Spark plugs*	AGSF-22FM1

* Refer to Vehicle Emissions Control Information (VECI) decal for spark plug gap information.

OCTANE RECOMMENDATIONS

Your vehicle is designed to use "Premium" unleaded gasoline with an (R+M)/2 octane rating  of 91 or higher for optimum performance. The use of gasolines with lower octane ratings may degrade performance. We do not recommend the use of gasolines labeled as "Premium" in high altitude areas that are sold with octane ratings of less than 91.

If your engine knocks under most driving conditions while you are using fuel with the recommended octane rating, see your dealer or a qualified service technician to prevent any engine damage.

4.6L DOHC SUPERCHARGED V–8 ENGINE

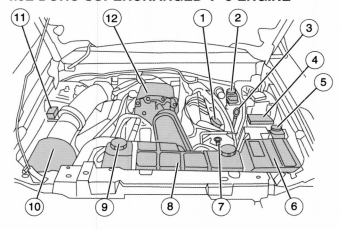

1. Engine oil filler cap
2. Brake fluid reservoir
3. Engine oil dipstick
4. Power distribution box
5. Windshield washer fluid reservoir
6. Battery
7. Power steering fluid reservoir
8. Engine coolant reservoir
9. Intercooler reservoir
10. Air filter assembly
11. Auxiliary power distribution block
12. Supercharger

SPORT INSTRUMENT CLUSTER

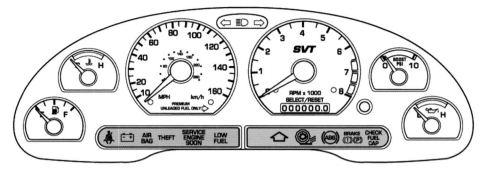

Lumbar and adjustable bolster controls

The lumbar and adjustable bolster controls are located on the front right corner of the driver seat. The power lumbar feature creates lower back support for the driver and may be adjusted to increase or decrease the support. The seat back and seat cushion bolsters inflate or deflate, allowing the driver to create a firmer or more loose fitting seat. Before adjusting these features, ensure that the seat is in the driving position, then:

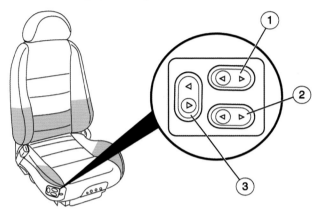

1. Seat back bolsters — Press ◀ to deflate (decrease firmness), press ▶ to inflate (increase firmness).

2. Seat cushion bolsters — Press ◀ to deflate (decrease firmness), press ▶ to inflate (increase firmness).

3. Lumbar controls — Press ◀ to inflate (increase lumbar support), or ▶ to deflate (decrease lumbar support.)

For maximum ease of vehicle ingress/egress, the seat cushion and seat back bolsters should be completely deflated.

⚠ **WARNING**

Children Can Be KILLED or INJURED by Passenger Air Bag.

The back seat is the safest place for children 12 and under. Make sure all children use seat belts or child seats.

TO BE REMOVED BY CUSTOMER ONLY

SAFETY ADVICE

Ford and Nick Jr.'s Blues Clues have teamed up to educate kids and parents about safety. Join us at www.clueintosafety.com for fun safety games and lessons.

This card highlights some important automobile safety practices.

See Owner Guide for further instructions.

With children, it may not be possible to get a proper fit using adult safety belts alone.

That is why child safety seats and boosters are so important.

Boost America!

Children 12 and under should always be properly restrained in the rear seat whenever possible.

KEEP THIS CARD IN GLOVE BOX

Ford Motor Company

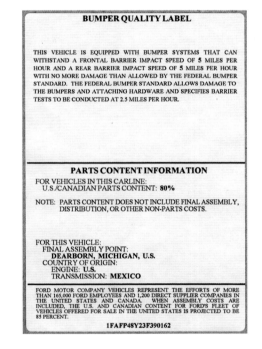

BUMPER QUALITY LABEL

THIS VEHICLE IS EQUIPPED WITH BUMPER SYSTEMS THAT CAN WITHSTAND A FRONTAL BARRIER IMPACT SPEED OF **5 MILES PER HOUR** AND A REAR BARRIER IMPACT SPEED OF **5 MILES PER HOUR** WITH NO MORE DAMAGE THAN ALLOWED BY THE FEDERAL BUMPER STANDARD. THE FEDERAL BUMPER STANDARD ALLOWS DAMAGE TO THE BUMPERS AND ATTACHING HARDWARE AND SPECIFIES BARRIER TESTS TO BE CONDUCTED AT 2.5 MILES PER HOUR.

PARTS CONTENT INFORMATION

FOR VEHICLES IN THIS CARLINE:
U.S./CANADIAN PARTS CONTENT: **80%**

NOTE: PARTS CONTENT DOES NOT INCLUDE FINAL ASSEMBLY, DISTRIBUTION, OR OTHER NON-PARTS COSTS.

FOR THIS VEHICLE:
FINAL ASSEMBLY POINT:
DEARBORN, MICHIGAN, U.S.
COUNTRY OF ORIGIN:
ENGINE: **U.S.**
TRANSMISSION: **MEXICO**

FORD MOTOR COMPANY VEHICLES REPRESENT THE EFFORTS OF MORE THAN 165,000 FORD EMPLOYEES AND 1,200 DIRECT SUPPLIER COMPANIES IN THE UNITED STATES AND CANADA. WHEN ASSEMBLY COSTS ARE INCLUDED, THE U.S. AND CANADIAN CONTENT FOR FORD'S FLEET OF VEHICLES OFFERED FOR SALE IN THE UNITED STATES IS PROJECTED TO BE 85 PERCENT.

1FAFP48Y23F390162

JACK USAGE AND STOWAGE
SEE OWNER GUIDE FOR DETAILED INSTRUCTIONS

JACKING INSTRUCTIONS:
1. Set parking brake. Automatic transmission: Place gear selection lever in "P" position. Manual transmission: Place gear shift lever in reverse. Turn off the engine and block the wheel diagonally opposite the flat tire.

⚠ **WARNING**
DO NOT ATTEMPT TO JACK CAR EXCEPT ON A LEVEL SURFACE.

SVT Cobra Independent Rear Suspension

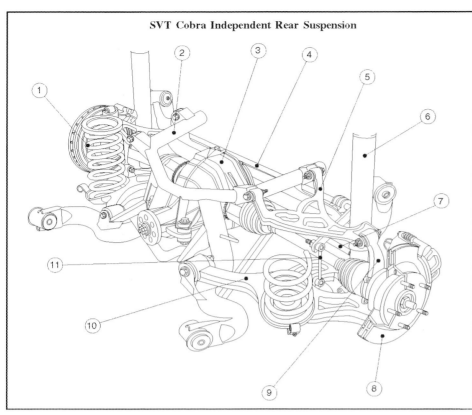

Item	Description		Item	Description
1	Linear rate coil spring		7	Tie rod
2	Tubular steel subframe		8	11.65 in rear rotor
3	3.55:1 limited slip differential		9	Aluminum alloy spindle
4	Tubular stabilizer bar		10	Aluminum alloy lower control arm
5	Steel upper control arm		11	Stabilizer bar link
6	Gas charged shock absorber			

SVT Cobra Front Suspension with Bilstein Gas-Charged Struts

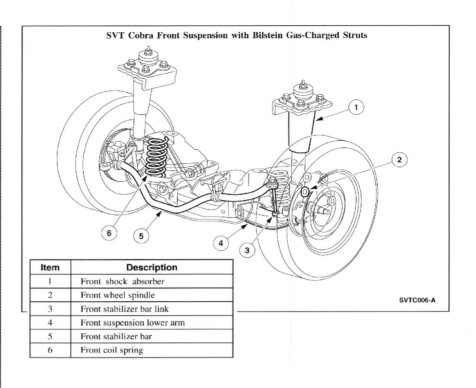

SVTC006-A

Item	Description
1	Front shock absorber
2	Front wheel spindle
3	Front stabilizer bar link
4	Front suspension lower arm
5	Front stabilizer bar
6	Front coil spring

Intercooler System

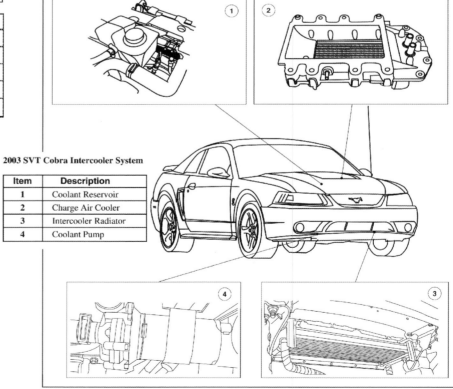

2003 SVT Cobra Intercooler System

Item	Description
1	Coolant Reservoir
2	Charge Air Cooler
3	Intercooler Radiator
4	Coolant Pump

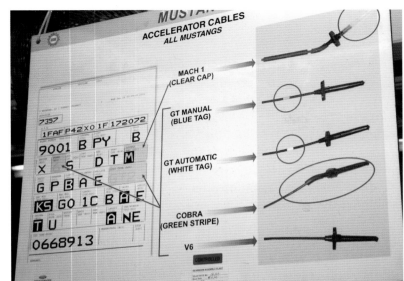

ACCELERATOR CABLES
ALL MUSTANGS

MACH 1
(CLEAR CAP)

GT MANUAL
(BLUE TAG)

GT AUTOMATIC
(WHITE TAG)

COBRA
(GREEN STRIPE)

V6

7357

1FAFP42X01F172072

9001 BPY B
X S DTM
GPBAE
KS GO 1C BAE
TU ANE
0668913

COBRA
SPEED CONTROL / THROTTLE CABLE ROUTING

Speed Control Cable - FRONT

Throttle Cable - REAR

Speed Control Cable - FRONT

Throttle Cable - REAR

DEARBORN ASSEMBLY PLANT

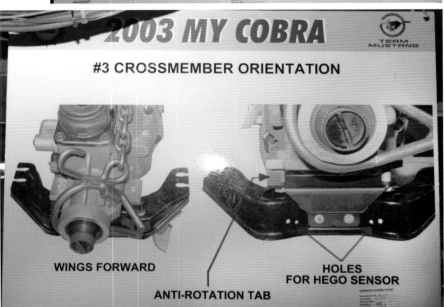

2003 MY COBRA

#3 CROSSMEMBER ORIENTATION

WINGS FORWARD

HOLES
FOR HEGO SENSOR

ANTI-ROTATION TAB

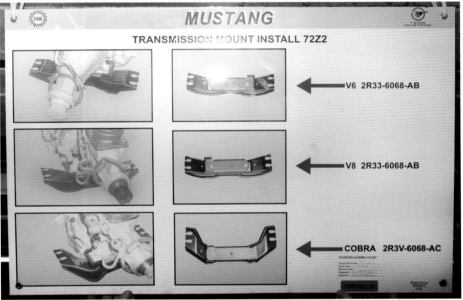

MUSTANG
TRANSMISSION MOUNT INSTALL 72Z2

V6 2R33-6068-AB

V8 2R33-6068-AB

COBRA 2R3V-6068-AC

MUSTANG
BASE HOOD

Part # 3r33-16612-CA

MUSTANG
HOOD - COBRA

PART# 2R3V-16612-A

Throughout Dearborn Assembly Plant, large color reference sheets provided background to workers and clearly highlighted notable differences between the Cobra and other Mustangs.
Photos: Marcie Cipriani, Frank Moriarty

151

BIRTH OF A COBRA

Shortly before the last Mustang rolled off the Dearborn Assembly Plant line in May of 2004, Frank Moriarty, the author of *Iron Fist, Lead Foot*, and designer Marcie Cipriani had the rare opportunity to witness beginning-to-end assembly of a 2004 SVT Mustang Cobra, a Screaming Yellow convertible assembled on March 18, 2004. What follows is a selection of memorable moments and key steps in the Birth of a Cobra.

Photos: Marcie Cipriani, Frank Moriarty

ENGINE BUILD

Romeo Engine Plant Niche Line
Romeo, Michigan

This one-time tractor manufacturing complex was re-christened Ford Romeo Engine Plant in 1990 and began producing high-volume passenger vehicle engines. The plant's Niche Line was responsible for SVT Cobra engines.

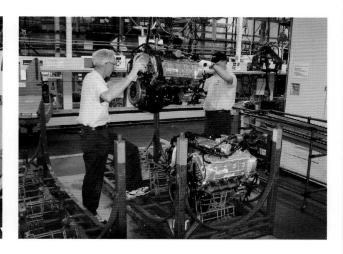

FINAL ASSEMBLY

Dearborn Assembly Plant
Dearborn, Michigan

Rising along the banks of the River Rouge in Dearborn, Michigan, the Dearborn Assembly Plant was the constantly-beating heart of the Ford River Rouge complex during nearly eight decades of automotive production.

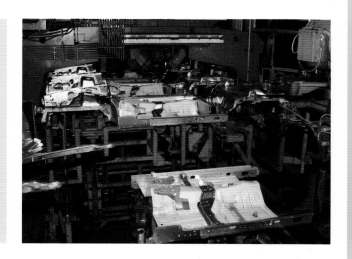

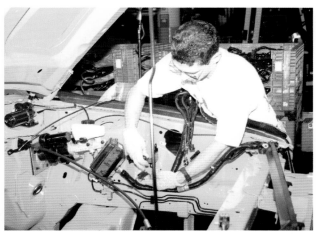

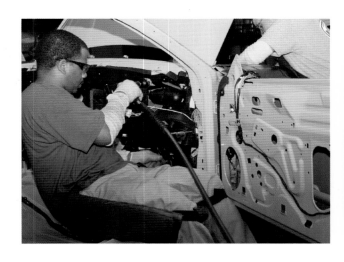

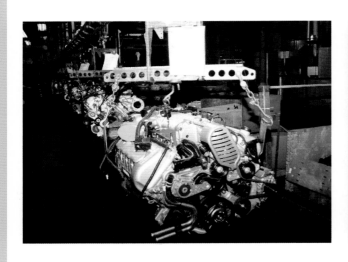
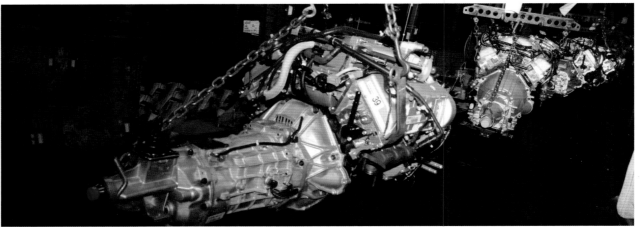

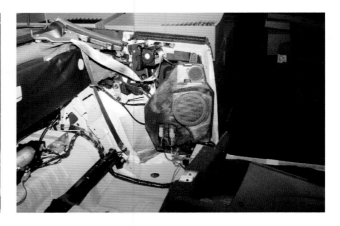

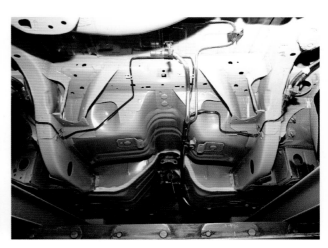

A proud moment in the history of SVT: the hard work is done, and the team
gathers as the 2003 Ford SVT Mustang Cobra is ready to be shown to the
world. The air of confidence over how well the Terminator would be received
was fully justified, as everyone who'd put countless hours of hard work into
this car knew that this was a Mustang for the ages.
Photo: Ford Motor Company